As one of the world's ____ ished
____ ands,
____ avel.

____ our
____ rets
____ rld,
____ of
____ el.

Rely on Thomas Cook as your
travelling companion on your next trip
and benefit from our unique heritage.

Thomas Cook **pocket** guides

PRAGUE

Written by Carolyn Zukowski
Updated by Kristina Konikova

Published by Thomas Cook Publishing
A division of Thomas Cook Tour Operations Limited
Company registration No: 3772199 England
The Thomas Cook Business Park, 9 Coningsby Road
Peterborough PE3 8SB, United Kingdom
Email: books@thomascook.com, Tel: +44 (0)1733 416477
www.thomascookpublishing.com

Produced by The Content Works Ltd
Aston Court, Kingsmead Business Park, Frederick Place
High Wycombe, Bucks HP11 1LA
www.thecontentworks.com

Series design based on an original concept by Studio 183 Limited

ISBN: 978-1-84848-312-5

First edition © 2006 Thomas Cook Publishing
This third edition © 2010 Thomas Cook Publishing
Text © Thomas Cook Publishing
Maps © Thomas Cook Publishing/PCGraphics (UK) Limited
Transport map © Communicarta Limited

Project Editor: Kelly Pipes
Production/DTP: Steven Collins

Printed and bound in Spain by GraphyCems

Cover photography (Astronomical Clock, Old Town Hall) © Peter M. Wilson/Alamy

CONTENTS

SYMBOLS KEY

The following symbols are used throughout this book:

ⓐ address ☎ telephone ⓦ website address ⏰ opening times
ⓝ public transport connections ❶ important

The following symbols are used on the maps:

ℹ️	information office	▦	points of interest
✈	airport	○	city
✚	hospital	○	large town
🛡	police station	○	small town
🚌	bus station	≈	motorway
🚆	railway station	—	main road
Ⓜ	metro	—	minor road
✝	cathedral	—	railway
❶	numbers denote featured cafés & restaurants		

Hotels and restaurants are graded by approximate price as follows:
£ budget price ££ mid-range price £££ expensive

The following abbreviations are used for addresses:
nábř.   nábřeží (embankment)
nám.   náměstí (square)
ul.   ulice (street)

▶ *The fairytale turrets of Týn Church*

INTRODUCING
Prague

Introduction

Think of DisneyWorld®, with its colourful attractions, fun houses, quaint miniature squares and breathtaking amusement rides. Now take away the carefully orchestrated customer service, cut the price of an entrance ticket in half, add lots of alcohol and cigarettes, and put a bureaucrat in control. It sounds absurd, but that's Prague (*Praha* in Czech). And it's precisely what has attracted artists, alchemists, anarchists and travellers to Prague for centuries.

While Prague's classical music and the Czech Republic's unmatched beer are among some of the best reasons to visit, the primary pleasure for many is simply strolling Prague's moody cobblestone streets and enjoying the unique atmosphere, rain or shine. Exquisite examples of a thousand years of European architecture are crammed together on the twisting narrow streets of a city that many travellers regard as 'the Europe that I wanted to see when I came to Europe'.

To limit uncontrolled development and to ensure that Prague retains its picture-perfect beauty for centuries to come, the City of Prague declared the core of the city the Prague Heritage Reserve. In 1992, UNESCO declared the city centre a World Heritage Site. With the inclusion of the Czech Republic into the EU in 2004, being a tourist here couldn't be easier or more satisfying.

It's fitting that the word *práh*, in Czech, means threshold. Prague is the gateway to the centre of Europe, bridging the gap between old and new. As you sit among the throngs of tables in Staroměstské náměstí (Old Town Square) you will witness the absurd minutiae of daily life – the supermodel who serves you at the hot-dog stand, the medieval-costumed minstrels talking on their mobile phones, or the artistic splash of graffiti on a Romanesque building. Prague's open-door policy couldn't be more apparent. So keep your eyes open and enjoy the ride. You will be coming back for more.

🔺 Prague, a graceful collision of old and new

When to go

There's no one single time of the year when you should or shouldn't head for Prague. The city has a completely different face in every season of the year. Don't think Prague is automatically at its best in summer; the bracing winter, blossom-coated spring and hazy autumn are romantic and colourful times to be in the city.

SEASONS & CLIMATE

Prague's geographical location in the northern part of central Europe allows for some mercurial weather patterns. This of course only adds to the attraction of this beautiful city. The average temperature in December and January is 5°C (41°F). In the hottest months, June and July, the temperature usually hovers at around 30°C (86°F).

ANNUAL EVENTS

There is always something happening in Prague. Here is a list of yearly events, but check Ⓦ www.pis.cz for the most current schedule in English. You can buy tickets in advance online for many of these at **Ticketpro** (Ⓦ www.ticketpro.cz).

Spring

One World International Film Festival (early March) One of Europe's leading human rights festivals. Ⓦ www.jedensvet.cz

Febiofest (late March) Now the largest audiovisual showcase in Central Europe, the week-long independent film festival features more than 500 movies in 15 cinemas around Prague. Ⓦ www.febiofest.cz

Velikonoce (Easter) On Easter Monday, boys carefully weave a willow switch and give their girlfriends a swat with it, thereby ensuring their health and beauty for the coming year. The girls, in exchange, give the boys a painted egg, or a swatch of ribbon to tie onto their willow switch.

Summer

Prague Spring Music Festival (12 May–4 June) Symphony, opera and chamber performances bring some of the world's best talent to Prague. Tickets are available in advance (beginning in December) from Ticketpro (see opposite) and online at Ⓦ www.festival.cz.

Český Pivní Festival (Czech Beer Festival) Exactly what its name implies. Ⓦ www.ceskypivnifestival.cz

Khamoro (late May) If you like to dance hard, this festival of gypsy culture is for you. Ⓦ www.khamoro.cz

Dance Prague June sees this international festival of contemporary dance. Ⓦ www.ifbbohemia.cz

Shakespeare Summer Festivities (June–Sept) The Burgrave Palace setting in the Prague Castle complex (see page 98) brings these plays to life. Ⓦ www.shakespeare.cz

Dvořákova Praha A three-week festival of classical music starting in mid-August – Dvorak fans will be in heaven. Concerts take place in the Rudolfinum. Ⓦ www.dvorakovapraha.cz

Autumn

Festival VyšeHrátky (early Sept) Marionettes and their masters make this one of the most wonderfully creepy events in Prague. Ⓦ www.vysehratky.cz

Strings of Autumn (Sept–Nov) This classical music festival draws heavily on the relationship of music and theatre, with famous personalities thrown in for good measure. Ⓦ www.strunypodzimu.cz

Anniversary of the Velvet Revolution (17 Nov) Watch the president place a wreath at the small bronze 'free hands' monument on the wall near Národní třída 20.

International Jazz Festival (late Nov) A celebration of jazz, held in venues across town. Ⓦ www.jazzfestivalpraha.cz

🔺 *A wintry view from the Prague Castle steps*

Winter

Advent & Christmas (5–26 Dec) St Mikuláš, the Czech version of St Nick, gives sweets to good children and coal to naughty ones; adults can expect grilled carp and hot mulled grog in abundance.

New Year's Eve (31 Dec) Give the embattled centre of Prague a miss during the New Year's Eve festivities, and go for spectacular views of fireworks and a mellower pace at Pražský hrad (Prague Castle, see page 98) or Vyšehrad (see page 112).

Prague Winter Festival (first week Jan) Seven days of classical music served up in some of Prague's most sumptuous interiors.
ⓦ www.praguewinterfestival.com

PUBLIC HOLIDAYS

Nový rok (New Year's Day) 1 Jan

Velikonoční pondělí (Easter Monday) 25 Apr 2011, 9 Apr 2012, 1 Apr 2013

Svátek práce (Labour Day) 1 May

Den osvobození (Liberation Day) 8 May

Den Cyrila a Metoděje (SS Cyril and Methodius) 5 July

Den upálení mistra Jana Husa (Jan Hus Day) 6 July

Den české státnosti (Czech Statehood Day) 28 Sept

Den vzniku Československa (Independence Day) 28 Oct

**Den boje za svobodu a demokracii
(Struggle for Freedom & Democracy Day)** 17 Nov

Štědrý den (Christmas Eve) 24 Dec

1. svátek vánoční (Christmas Day) 25 Dec

2. svátek vánoční (Boxing Day) 26 Dec

Tapping the market

It's the classic David and Goliath tale, with a little globalisation thrown in. *Budějovické*, or *Budweis* (in German) beer comes from the Czech city of České Budějovice, where it has been brewed since the 13th century. In 1876, 19 years before the Czech company, Budvar, began bottling in České Budějovice, a German-born American immigrant, Adolphus Busch, started to produce his Budweiser beer in St Louis. Busch declared the product the King of Beers, and registered the trademark Budweiser in the US.

There was no problem until both companies started looking to sell their product internationally and clashed at a trade fair at the turn of the 20th century. In 1911 they came to an understanding; Budvar agreed not to sell their beer north of the Panama Canal and Budweiser agreed to stay out of Europe. This worked well until the

fall of the Berlin wall, when the possibility of breaking into new international markets became appealing to both sides.

'We have no problem with Budvar selling their beer. They just can't use names too close to ours', say the Budweiser execs in the US. The Czech Budvar team retorts: '*Budějovické* (*Budweis*) has been producing beer since 1260; before the US even existed!' Neither company relishes the prospect of consumers mistaking their product as something produced by the other, though the dispute is probably helping the much smaller Budvar more than hindering it. Budvar admits that the long-running battle has had a beneficial effect, defining its brand strategy and enabling it to tap new markets that otherwise might have been much harder to penetrate by keeping the brand fresh in people's minds and giving them something to talk about in the pub. A case of any publicity is good publicity.

⬤ *Roll out the barrel*

History

The city of Prague has been influenced, and at times overrun, by people from all points of the compass, including Celts, Slavs, Italians, Poles, Jews, Germans and Russians, to name a few. Communists and capitalists as well as hundreds of artists, alchemists and architects have left their mark on 'the city of a hundred spires', 'the new Left Bank' and 'the Bohemian capital'.

In the mid-14th century, Prague was the centre of the Holy Roman Empire and Europe's third-largest city in terms of population. The reign of Charles IV was a Golden Age in Czech history, but its end brought economic and political strife to the area as Protestant Hussites – inspired by the ideas of the religious reformer Jan Hus – battled it out with crusaders sent by the Catholic Church in the 15th century.

The Austrian Habsburgs captured the Bohemian throne in the 16th century, which left Bohemia as part of the Austrian Empire for 400 long and sombre years, until the end of World War I. The Habsburgs were repressive rulers, except for the brief but bright reign of the mentally unstable Emperor Rudolf II. He surrounded himself with gifted astronomers such as Tycho Brahe and Johannes Kepler, while alchemists such as John Dee stirred mysterious vats in the castle kitchens and exotic animals strolled through the corridors.

At the end of the 18th century, the Enlightenment

○ *Architectural detail in St Vitus Cathedral*

reforms of Maria Theresa and her son, Josef II, led to the Germanisation of the country. It wasn't long before the Czechs began to express their desire for self-determination. The Czech National Revival movement was born, and aspired to reintroduce Czech language and culture; it soon began to strive for political emancipation as well.

On 28 October 1918, an independent Czech and Slovak state was formed in Prague after the Austro-Hungarian defeat in World War I. This new country, led by President Tomáš Garrigue Masaryk, experienced a boom and Czechoslovakia became one of the ten richest nations in the world.

The Nazi occupation of Bohemia and Moravia was disastrous for Czechoslovakia, leaving only the country's beautiful buildings unscathed. After World War II, the restored Czechoslovak Republic fell under Soviet influence. An attempt to reform and humanise the Communist system, known as the Prague Spring, failed miserably when Russian forces invaded the country in August 1968. The 1970s and 1980s were stifled times for many Czechoslovaks, who created their own dissident counter-culture.

Mass protests and demonstrations in Prague led to the bloodless overthrow of the Communist regime in November 1989, also known as the Velvet Revolution. On 1 January 1993, because of 'irreconcilable differences', the Czechoslovak state was divided into independent Czech and Slovak republics. Years of financial mismanagement left the city in disrepair, and capitalists soon took on the task of renovating it to its former beauty.

After joining the European Union in 2004, the Czech economy boomed significantly and remained relatively healthy even during the global financial crisis of 2008-9. With confidence still high, the country is now working towards adopting the euro within the next five to eight years.

Lifestyle

The Czech population is incredibly diverse, from tram-riding *babičkas* (grannies) wearing headscarves to Zen youths eating macrobiotic dishes at one of Prague's new organic restaurants. A few decades ago, the city lost many of its skilled hopefuls to emigration but, over the last few years, an influx of immigrants

● *Staré Město after a few beers*

and returning Czech emigrants has made Prague more interesting than ever. Many Czechs have a German, Hungarian, Polish, Romany, Slovak or Vietnamese background.

This mix of nationalities and ancestries means that Czechs are generally very welcoming to foreigners. Particularly in Prague itself, there is an atmosphere of inclusiveness and multiculturalism that extends not only to foreign visitors and immigrants but to people of all races, abilities and sexualities. Due to the high number of tourists, residents of Prague are well used to foreigners and many speak some English. In the more rural areas you may encounter a bit more curiosity.

The Czechs are generally well educated and seem to have a better grasp of mathematics, history and world geography than their similarly educated European counterparts. In Prague you will find many young people who are very eager to practise their English. There is also a general aptitude and affinity for music and art, resulting in some imaginative graffiti and fantastic impromptu musical performances in pubs.

During the hot months of summer, you may find that there aren't that many Czechs around. Don't take it personally; Czechs often leave their apartments in the city for their *chata* or *chaloupka* in the country at the weekends. These tiny country houses are a great way to take advantage of the beautiful countryside. Many Czechs are great gardeners and nature enthusiasts, knowing which wild mushrooms are edible, and exactly which part of a slaughtered pig is the tastiest.

When in Prague, bear in mind that your holiday represents a luxury that the average citizen, earning around 23,000 Kč a month, does not have. Remarking loudly 'Wow, this (fill in the blank with: beer, knick-knack, bus trip, meal) is SO CHEAP!' is perhaps not the most sensitive approach. What you may consider cheap is, for many Czechs, still out of reach.

Culture

For a city of little more than one million inhabitants, Prague packs in enough museums, art galleries, theatres and opera houses to provide a lifetime of entertainment.

Prague has a proud history of supporting culture. It's a city of artistic innovation and tolerance, and has provided appreciative audiences to musicians such as Mozart and writers like Franz Kafka. The most important cultural landmark in Prague is the Národní divadlo (National Theatre, see page 78). Built at the birth of the Czechoslovak nation, when there was a need to create a national identity using Czech language, music and drama, the theatre represented the cultural life Czechs wanted for themselves. Today the National Theatre oversees three ensembles: the **Státní Opera** (National Opera ⓐ Legerova 75 ⓣ 296 117 111 ⓦ www.opera.cz), the National Ballet and the National Drama Company, which perform at some of the most beautiful venues in town, namely the National Theatre (see page 78), Estates Theatre (see page 70) and **Kolowrat Theatre** (ⓐ Ovocný trh 6).

Prague Spring Music Festival (see page 9) is Prague's best-known annual cultural event, where the festival venues are as big a draw as the music. It begins on 12 May, the anniversary of the composer Bedřich Smetana's death, with a procession from his grave at Vyšehrad, followed by a performance of his *Má vlast* song cycle.

For a typically Czech theatrical experience, you can choose from three distinctive performance genres, all of which are great for visitors, as they are language-free and held at central locations. Visually stunning 'black light theatre' stories are told using elements of mime, modern dance, ballet, animated film, and acting or puppetry bathed in light on a dark background. Marionette theatre is another

● *Marionette theatre is a delightful Czech tradition*

Czech tradition, offering wonderful puppet performances ranging from Mozart's famous *Don Giovanni* to the Beatles' *Yellow Submarine*. *Laterna Magika* is a uniquely Czech mix of film, visual effects, sound and ballet. Always evolving, the themes are fresh and exciting, and performances are well worth the entrance ticket.

The Czech film tradition embodies the history of the Czech Republic: rise, repression, rebellion and rebirth. Prague's **Film & Television School of the Academy of Performing Arts** (🅐 Na Poříčí 26 ☎ 221 716 333 🌐 www.divadloarcha.cz 🕐 Box office: 10.00–18.00 Mon–Fri; until 20.00 on performance days) and the **Barrandov Studios** (🅐 Krizeneckeho nam. 322/5 ☎ 267 071 122 🌐 www.barrandov.com) have a long and distinguished history. They produced some 80 films a year from the 1930s until the Soviet invasion in August 1968. Privatised after the fall of Communism, Barrandov Studios no longer receives funding from the government.

Encouraged by the classic films of Czech producers Jan Svěrak and Jan Hřebejk, including Svěrak's Oscar-winning *Kolya* and Hřebejk's *Divided We Fall*, more recent Czech film-makers have started to make waves: look out for *Tobruk* by Václav Marhoul and Tomás Barina's *Bobule*.

Now, foreign film-makers have discovered Prague as an attractive location due to its beautiful surroundings, undamaged architecture, relatively low filming costs and expert local crews. To support the growing number of foreign film projects, local production companies as well as agencies providing casting, lighting, editing and special effects services have been established. Some Prague cinemas now show Czech films with English subtitles, so it's worth going to see one while you're in the city.

▶ *A view from the Vltava towards Prague Castle*

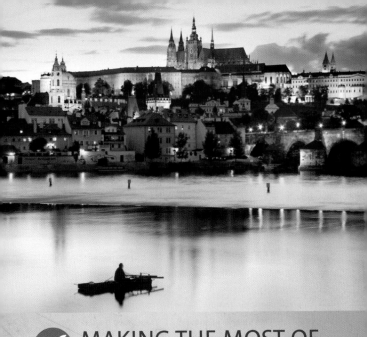

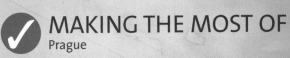 MAKING THE MOST OF
Prague

Shopping

Prague's mix of high-end fashion, low-brow kitsch and home-grown market stalls holds appeal for just about everyone, but if you want to buy luxury clothing or electronics, you will probably find them cheaper at home. For antiques buffs, Prague has dozens of antiquarian book shops that can yield some excellent finds. Many *bazars* (second-hand shops) have interesting supplies of old linens, mirrors, brooches and crystal beads.

Nearly every *papírnictví* (stationery shop) has beautiful watercolour and coloured-chalk sets that make perfect gifts. Other top trinkets include small bottles of emerald green absinthe, Bohemian crystal, colourful necklaces, funky (and occasionally tacky) nesting dolls, garnet jewellery and ceramic goods.

The main shopping areas are pedestrianised Na příkopě, at the foot of Václavské náměstí (Wenceslas Square, see page 62), lined with mid-range international retailers, and Národní (National)

⬤ *Na příkopě dressed for winter celebrations*

Street. Celetná is the souvenir strip, while the area between the Old Town Square (see page 66) and Karlův most (Charles Bridge, see page 94) is packed with small, winding streets that contain the city's highest concentration of shops. Check out Charles Bridge itself, where you'll find quirky, small kiosks.

There are two permanent markets in Prague: Havelské tržiště (Havel's Market, see page 72), the main open-air market in Old Town featuring a good selection of fruit and vegetables, artwork, leather goods, flowers, wooden toys and ceramics; and **Pražská Tržnice** (ⓐ Holešovice ⓛ 07.00–20.00 Mon–Sat ⓝ Metro: Vltavská, then tram: Pražská Tržnice), with outdoor market stalls that sell just about everything. Both attract a large crowd of locals and tourists. Haggling is best left until the end of the day, when the sellers are more receptive to offers.

USEFUL SHOPPING PHRASES

What time do the shops open/close?
Kdy otevírají/zavírají obchody?
Gdee ohteveerahyee/zavveerayee obkhodee?

How much is this?
Kolik to stojí?
Kollick toh stoyee?

Can I try this on?
Můžu si to vyzkoušet?
Moozhoo see toh veezkowshett?

My size is ...
Moje velikost je ...
Moye vellickost yeh ...

I'll take this one, thank you
Vezmu toto, děkuji
Vezmoo totoh, dyekooyee

Eating & drinking

Pivo (beer) is the lifeblood of this metropolis, and you'll be hard-pressed to find anyone who doesn't imbibe the occasional half-litre. The beer-drinking tradition started in the Middle Ages, a direct response to water pollution; brewing and filtering the beer seemed to kill off most of the bugs. Today, Czech beer has an alcohol level of between 3.5 and 5 per cent and people stick to their favourite brands, swearing lifelong allegiance to the pub that serves it. A beer has to look just right when it comes to you, with a thick, frothy head, and it must be cool, not cold. A proper Pilsner takes seven minutes to pour. The best brands are Bernard, Gambrinus, Kozel, Pilsner Urquell, Staropramen and Radegast. To really feel at home in Prague, you need learn just one simple phrase: *Ještě jedno pivo prosím* ('One more beer, please').

If you choose to eat in a pub rather than a tourist restaurant, you'll probably spend no more than 300 Kč (around £10) for your soup, main course and drink. Try *svíčková*, a dish of tender beef covered in an orange cream sauce topped with cranberries, cream and a slice of lemon. Bread dumplings often accompany the meal and the trick is not to leave one speck of sauce. For vegetarians, *smažený sýr* (fried cheese) is good with chips and tartare sauce and sometimes even a bit of greenery. If you want a really cheap meal on the go, try a *párek v rohlíku* (hot dog with ketchup and/or mustard) or a *langoš* (fried

PRICE CATEGORIES

The restaurant price guides given in this book indicate the approximate cost of a three-course dinner without drinks.

£ up to 300 Kč   ££ 300–500 Kč   £££ 500–700 Kč

🔺 *Beer is the national drink; Pilsner Urquell has been brewed since 1842*

dough with garlic, cheese or cinnamon sugar on top). You can find fast-food kiosks on just about any street corner in Prague.

Czech cuisine does not offer much choice for vegetarians, but the situation is improving and most people will probably find at least a couple of filling dishes to their liking, including *bramboračka* (potato soup), *ovocné knedlíky* (fruit-filled dumplings with cream or sweet cottage cheese) or *jablečný závin* (apple strudel). Czech cooking and eating habits have been shifting towards a healthier lifestyle, but traditional Czech recipes with their rich sauces and condiments are still extremely popular. If this isn't your cup of tea, then don't despair; Prague has some good organic, vegetarian and ethnic restaurants. Check the listings in the *Prague Post* (ⓦ www.praguepost.com) for the latest reviews.

As for drinks, if you're not in the mood for beer, you can have *minerálka* (mineral water), *pomerančový džus* (orange juice) or *jablečný džus* (apple juice). Czechs also like to drink *čaj* (tea) and *káva* (coffee), with or without *mléko* (milk) or *smetana* (cream). For a treat, sip a *slivovice* (plum) or *meruňkovice* (apricot) Moravian brandy.

Most restaurants in Prague have a menu in English. The expected tip for good service is between 5 and 10 per cent, but if you get the typically Czech 'service with a scowl', you can forget the tip.

There are numerous supermarkets in Prague if you prefer picnicking to eating in restaurants, but it's much more interesting to visit a local *potraviny* (grocery) and pick up some *šunka* (ham), *salám* (salami) or *sýr* (cheese) for your alfresco sandwich. For bread, you can usually choose between fresh *rohlíky* (small white bread baguettes) or *chleba* (rye or whole wheat bread). If you want butter, ask for *máslo*.

Please note that some venues – including restaurants, clubs, bars and even shops – have fairly irregular opening hours. If you're intending to visit a particular place, it's best to phone before leaving to make sure they'll be open.

USEFUL DINING PHRASES

I would like a table for ... people
Přeji si stůl pro ... osob
Przheyee see stool proh ... ossobb

May I have the bill, please?
Přeji si zaplatit, prosím?
Przeyee see zaplatteet, prosseem?

Could I have it well-cooked/medium/rare, please?
Přeji si to dobře propečené/středně/jen lehce propečené,
prosím?
*Przeyee see toh dobrzeh proppecheneh/strzednyeh/yen lehtseh
proppecheneh, prosseem?*

I am a vegetarian. Does this contain meat?
Jsem vegetarián. Není v tom maso?
Ysem vegetahreeahn. Nenyee ftom mahsoh?

Where is the toilet please?
Kde je záchod, prosím vás?
Gdeh yeh zahkhod, prosseem vahs?

I would like a cup of/two cups of/another coffee/tea
Přeji si šálek/dva šálky/ještě jednu kávu/ještě jeden čaj
*Przeyee see shahleck/dvah shalckee/yeshtye yednoo kahvoo/
yeshtye yedenn chay*

Entertainment & nightlife

Prague has over 30 *kino* (cinemas), some showing international films, some showing Czech films. Admission costs anything from 110 Kč to 200 Kč. Hollywood blockbusters may be dubbed into Czech, but films are usually shown in their original language; *v původním znění* means 'orginal soundtrack' (undubbed) and *české titulky* means 'Czech subtitles'.

The majority of Prague's dance clubs cater to the young MTV Europe crowd who want to hear techno/tribal beats. Most venues open late (after 21.00) and keep the music going until 04.00 or 05.00. But some of the most popular and interesting scenes in Prague are the alternative and experimental venues that combine theatres and clubs with an underground look and feel. There you'll find bands, DJs, drama, dance, art and films under one roof. Two of the best are the Roxy (see page 78) and the Palác Akropolis (see page 122).

Clubs are to be found all over Prague, but each area has its own certain style. For an upmarket tipple, try the Malá Strana area (see page 110), where jazz and cocktails mix with the lamplight and smoky alleyways. For a more eclectic mix of performance art while nuzzling your neighbour and guzzling beer, try Josefov (see page 93)

WHAT'S ON?

As soon as you hit town, buy the English-language weekly, *The Prague Post*, at any newspaper stand, sit down at a café and make your plan of attack. Its *Night & Day* section is thick with cultural offerings.

Rudolfinum Concert Hall

and the Old Town (see page 77). The glittery club scene is most attractive in the New Town (see page 77). For a night you won't remember, the Žižkov and Vinohrady areas (see page 123) have a great mix of places, ranging from grungy local hang-outs to sleekly designed gay and lesbian bars that stay open late and don't charge steep entry prices.

Along with the dedicated concert halls, Prague's many churches and baroque palaces also serve as performance venues, staging choral performances, organ recitals, and concerts by string quartets, brass ensembles and, occasionally, full orchestras. You can get details of these concerts from PIS (Prague Information Service) offices (see page 151). If you go to a concert in a church, remember to take an extra layer of clothing, even on a hot summer day.

For most events, even the ones that are officially 'sold out', you can often get tickets at the box office half an hour or so before show time. Most performances have a certain number of tickets set aside for VIP guests and visitors, so take a chance and you may be rewarded with the show of a lifetime. Most venues offer discounts for students, children and disabled visitors.

If you want to be sure of a seat, try a ticket agency. Their advantage is convenience; they accept credit cards and you can book from abroad using their website. Ticketpro (see page 8) is the biggest agency, with branches in PIS offices and many other places around town.

● *So much to see, so little time!*

Sport & relaxation

SPECTATOR SPORTS

Football AC Sparta Praha is one of the most successful football clubs in the country. Home games take place at the **Generali Arena** (ⓐ Milady Horákové 1066/98). For information on ticketing and stadium tours, call ❶ 296 111 400 or see ⓦ www.sparta.cz.

Ice hockey The HC Slavia Praha ice hockey team is world class and plays at the **O2 Arena** (ⓐ Ocelařska 2), previously known as Sazka. Call ❶ 267 311 417 or see ⓦ www.hc-slavia.cz for details. HC Sparta Praha is based at the multi-purpose **Tesla Arena** (ⓐ Za elektrarnou 419 ⓦ www.tesla-arena.cz or ⓦ www.hcsparta.cz). HC Rabat Kladno plays at the small **Zimní Stadion** (ⓐ Petra Bezruče 2531 ❶ 312 276 035 ⓦ www.hc-kladno.cz).

PARTICIPATION SPORTS

Tennis With tennis being the number one participation sport in Prague, you'll find a good choice of clubs and courts dotted around. One of the best is the **I. Český Lawn Tennis Klub** (ⓐ Ostrov Štvanice 38 ❶ 222 316 317 ⓦ www.cltk.cz ❹ 07.00–22.00), which has 14 outdoor and ten indoor courts available for public bookings until 15.00 on weekdays and all day at weekends. Otherwise, try contacting **Etennis** (ⓐ Povodňova 24 ❶ 602 357 316 ⓦ www.etennis.cz) or **Tennis Club Prague** (ⓐ Střelecky Ostrov 336 ❶ 774 613 444 ⓦ www.tennisprague.eu).

Boating Renting a rowing boat or pedalo on the Vltava River will give you a different perspective on the city. You'll find numerous boat rental agencies open every day from April to the end of October, from 09.00 to nightfall under Charles Bridge (see page 94) or on Slovanský Ostrov.

Cycling In the warmer months, rent a bicycle or try a guided cycling tour through the city. Two companies offer similar deals:

City Bike ⓐ Kralodvorska 5 ⓣ 776 180 284 ⓦ www.citybike-prague.com ⓛ Bike rental: 09.00–19.00 Apr–Oct; tours: 10.30, 13.30, 16.30

Praha Bike ⓐ Dlouhá 24 ⓣ 732 388 880 ⓦ www.prahabike.cz ⓛ Hours vary depending on season

RELAXATION

Walking tours On a walking tour of the city you will discover secret spots that you may never have seen without a guide. The **Sightseeing Expert** agency (ⓣ 776 100 006 ⓦ www.sightseeingexpert.com) offers a variety of interesting and themed tours including the four-hour Insider Tour, which covers most of the city's highlights and includes refreshments and a ride on the funicular. Insider Tours leave daily from the statue at the top of Václavské náměstí (Wenceslas Square, see page 62) at 13.30.

Prague Walks (ⓐ Jakubská 4 ⓣ 222 322 309 ⓦ www.praguewalks.com ⓝ Metro: Staroměstská) also has a good range of tour options, all leaving from the Staroměstská radnice (Old Town Hall, see page 65).

Gyms & spas Getting a massage or a spa treatment is still reasonably cheap in Prague. If your hotel doesn't have a fitness centre, there are various private options in the centre. Excellent venues in which to feel the burn and relish the post-blitz euphoria are:

Cybex Health Club & Spa ⓐ Prague Hilton, Pobřežní 1 ⓣ 224 842 375 ⓦ www.cybex-fitness.cz ⓛ 06.00–22.00 Mon–Fri, 07.00–22.00 Sat & Sun ⓝ Metro: Florenc

World Class Fitness Centre ⓐ Václavské nám. 22 ⓣ 234 699 100 ⓦ www.worldclassfitness.net ⓛ 07.30–21.00 ⓝ Metro: Muzeum

Accommodation

The bad news is that accommodation in the centre of Prague is no longer the cheap sleep that travellers bragged about ten years ago. The good news is that Prague's swift and reliable public transportation makes almost any out-of-the-way place an easy hop, skip and jump to the centre.

If you still wish to stay in the centre, the most conveniently located rooms are in the Old Town, Lesser Quarter and Hradčany (Castle District) – they command the best views with the biggest price tags. Old Town addresses can be less than peaceful due to revellers staggering home after a night out, so check the location of your accommodation or look at the room before making a commitment. The districts of New Town and Vyšehrad offer less pricey accommodation and are also convenient for the main sights.

Cheaper options are plentiful, whether you wish to stay in a *penzion*, hostel or camping ground. The word *penzion* means 'bed and breakfast accommodation', although the breakfast may consist of only coffee and rolls with butter. Some of the hostel-type accommodation will surprise you with modern facilities, good locations and friendly service. For nature-lovers, or those on a particularly tight budget, there are many camping sites around Prague. You can expect to spend 100–200 Kč a night for the right

PRICE CATEGORIES
The ratings below indicate the approximate cost of a double room including breakfast per person per night.
£ up to 500 Kč **££** 500–2,000 Kč **£££** 2,000–4,000 Kč

to pitch your tent, and about 350 Kč a night to park your caravan.

The hotel rating system in Prague is arbitrary, sometimes dictated by the accommodation owners rather than a controlling body, and the price that you pay does not always reflect the level of service or the quality of surroundings. For this reason, some visitors like to book their accommodation on arrival rather than pre-booking. It is worth remembering that if you arrive late in the

● *Andĕl's Hotel is ideally placed for shopping*

day, you can try asking for a discount on hotel or *penzion* rooms; these establishments would often rather let a room at a discount than have it go empty. If you want help finding what you're looking for, there are good accommodation-finding agencies in town. Two of the best are:

AVE ⓐ Hlavní nádráží (Main Train Station), Wilsonová 8
ⓣ 251 551 011; 24-hour late arrivals helpline: 602 180 312
ⓦ www.praguehotellocator.com

Prague Information Service (PIS) See page 151 for contact details and opening hours.

If you prefer to have your accommodation booked before you leave, AVE's website offers big internet discounts on some of the nicest hotels in town as well as on budget places to stay. For hostel and backpacker accommodation bookings, ⓦ www.hostelworld.com is an excellent site.

HOTELS

Anděl's Hotel ££ Modern and sleekly designed, right next to the Nový Smíchov shopping centre. ⓐ Stroupežnického 21, Smíchov (Malá Strana & Hradčany) ⓣ 296 889 688 ⓦ www.andelshotel.com
ⓜ Metro: Anděl

Botel Admiral ££ A boat hotel with some great views of the river and easy access to all the sights. ⓐ Hořejší nábř. 57, Smíchov (Malá Strana & Hradčany) ⓣ 257 321 302 ⓦ www.admiral-botel.cz ⓜ Metro: Anděl

Hotel Antik ££ Small, quiet and perfectly located 4-star hotel with lots of nice antique touches and a garden out the back. ⓐ Dlouha 22 (Staré Město & Nové Město) ⓣ 222 322 288 ⓦ www.hotelantik.cz
ⓜ Metro: Nám. Republiky or Staroměstská

◓ *The elegant and upmarket Hotel Paříž*

Mamaison Residences ££ Luxurious, fully equipped apartments in central locations throughout Prague. Office: ⓐ Janáčkovo nábřeží 15 ⓣ 225 994 611 or 234 705 111 Ⓦ www.mamaison.com

Castle Steps Hotel £££ Friendly, centrally located and as boutique as can be, located on the stairs to the castle and within walking distance of all the charming places in Malá Strana. ⓐ Nerudova 10 (Malá Strana & Hradčany) ⓣ 257 216 337 Ⓦ www.castlesteps.com Ⓝ Metro: Malostranská

Hotel Paříž £££ Classic art nouveau hotel close to all the main sights; worth the financial splurge. ⓐ Ul. Obecního domu 1 (Staré Město & Nové Město) ⓣ 222 195 195 Ⓦ www.hotel-pariz.cz Ⓝ Metro: Nám. Republiky

Questenberk Hotel £££ Housed in a former church with modest but tastefully furnished rooms and a location near the castle which has other hoteliers green with envy. ⓐ Úvoz 15 (Malá Strana & Hradčany) ⓣ 220 407 600 Ⓦ www.hotelq.cz Ⓝ Tram: 22 to Pohořelec

Radisson Blu Alcron Hotel £££ Central, nicely appointed, with barrier-free access, and all the expected 5-star perks. ⓐ Štěpánská 40 (Staré Město & Nové Město) ⓣ 222 820 000 Ⓦ www.radissonblu.com Ⓝ Metro: Můstek

HOSTELS

A Plus Hostel £ This very central hostel near the main coach station is a firm favourite. Breakfast is included in the price and there's internet access and a guest kitchen. ⓐ Na Florenci 1413/33

(Stare Město & Nove Město) ☎ 222 314 272 ⓦ www.aplus-hostel.cz
Ⓝ Metro: Florenc

Czech Inn £ If you thought hostelling was all about queuing for
a flooded bathroom and crusty socks on dusty dorm floors, think
again – this is a boutique hostel. It manages to be trendy and
cutting edge (including free Wi-Fi) while charging just a few hundred
crowns for a dorm bed. ⓐ Francouzská 76 (Vinohrady, Vyšehrad &
Žižkov) ☎ 267 267 600 ⓦ www.czech-inn.com Ⓝ Metro: Nám. Míru

Miss Sophie's £ Very comfortable, boutique backpackers' pad with
friendly staff, specially designed en suite rooms and a great location.
ⓐ Melounova 3 (Vinohrady, Vyšehrad & Žižkov) ☎ 296 303 530
ⓦ www.miss-sophies.com Ⓝ Metro: I. P. Pavlova

CAMPSITES

Intercamp Kotva £ Only 20 minutes from the centre of Prague,
with pitches for tents and hook-ups for caravans and all the
facilities you need. ⓐ U ledaren 1557/55, Braník ☎ 244 461 712
ⓦ www.kotvacamp.cz Ⓝ Tram: 3, 17 or 21 to Nádraží Braník,
then walk towards river following 'Camping' signs

Sunny Camp £ About 30 minutes from the centre of Prague, with
lots of green space for tents and caravans. The camp is signposted
and just 500 m (¼ mile) from the metro stop. ⓐ Smíchovská 1989,
Stodůlky ☎ 251 625 774 ⓦ www.sunny-camp.cz Ⓝ Metro: Lužiny

❶ Both camping sites can offer basic accommodation in their on-site
penzions if the weather makes sleeping in a tent seem unappealing.

THE BEST OF PRAGUE

A river meanders through Prague, and you will want to do the same. Even getting lost on a cobbled side street is part of the city's charm. The most important sights are centred around the Old Town. Just walking these streets, even if you flounder in the tourist current, will astound you. There are few cities as picture-perfect as Prague.

TOP 10 ATTRACTIONS

- **Václavské náměstí (Wenceslas Square)** The Czech Champs-Élysées and the biggest and busiest shopping plaza in Prague (see page 62)

- **Pražský hrad (Prague Castle)** Possibly the largest ancient castle complex in the world, boasting a magnificently elevated cliff-top position, and crammed with artistic and architectural treasures (see page 98)

- **Karlův most (Charles Bridge)** A vibrant place day or night, bustling with vendors, entertainers, locals and tourists (see page 94)

- **Obecní dům (Municipal House)** An art nouveau dream (see page 65)

- **Malá Strana (Lesser Quarter)** Ancient and atmospheric (see page 94)

- **Petřín Hill & funicular** A 318 m (1,043 ft) hill covered in eight parks and topped with a 62 m (203 ft) copy of the Eiffel Tower. It offers fabulous views of Prague and the surrounding area (see page 98)

- **Josefov (Jewish Quarter)** A spot for quiet reflection among some beautiful historic buildings (see page 80)

- **Staroměstské náměstí (Old Town Square)** Studded with cafés and inimitable baroque, Gothic, and Romanesque architecture, including the Old Town Hall and its exquisite 14th-century Astronomical Clock, St Nicolas Church, and the Jan Hus Monument (see page 66)

- **Národní muzeum (National Museum)** A bastion of Czech history and prehistory (see page 70)

- **Týn Church** Towering above Staroměstské náměstí (Old Town Square), the lopsided Gothic spires, symbolising the male and female elements, are a Prague landmark (see page 66)

🔽 *Prague's many bridges*

Suggested itineraries

HALF-DAY: PRAGUE IN A HURRY

If you have only a few hours to spare, then concentrate on Hradčany (the Castle District) and Malá Strana (the Lesser Quarter). Visit the Gothic Chrám sv. Vita (St Vitus Cathedral, see page 100) and Kostel sv. Jiří (St George's Basilica, see page 102), and pass the Lilliputian houses of Zlatá ulička (Golden Lane, see page 103). Then descend into Malá Strana, where you'll find ancient burgher houses and the baroque, copper-domed Chrám sv. Mikuláše (St Nicolas Church, see page 94). Making your way across Karlův most (Charles Bridge, see page 94) can take as little or as much time as you like; if you

● *St Vitus Cathedral – the perfect place for slaying a dragon*

enjoy souvenir stands, performers, artists, musicians, or just
beautiful city views, you may like to linger a while.

1 DAY: TIME TO SEE A LITTLE MORE

After a morning in the Hradčany and Malá Strana areas, make your
way from Karlův most (Charles Bridge) on the time- and tourist-
worn cobblestones to the oldest part of Prague, the aptly named
Staré Město (Old Town, see page 60). At its centre is the fabulous
Staroměstské náměstí (Old Town Square, see page 66), home to
some of Prague's most famous and beautiful monuments, such as
the colourful Orloj (Astronomical Clock, see page 65) and Týn Church
(see page 66). From there, work your way up Celetná ulice towards
the Prašná brána (Powder Tower, see page 65) and the Obecní dům
(Municipal House, see page 65), and from there, walk west along
Na příkopě to the tourist mecca that is Václavské náměstí
(Wenceslas Square, see page 62).

2–3 DAYS: TIME TO SEE MUCH MORE

With a bit more time, you'll be able to do everything listed above
in more depth, plus spend half a day in Josefov (Jewish Quarter, see
page 80), with its own pensive and reverent atmosphere. Then visit
a gallery or a museum, and maybe take in an evening concert. To keep
your energy levels up, sample some wonderfully heavy Czech cuisine
from one of the recommended local restaurants (see page 92).

LONGER: ENJOYING PRAGUE TO THE FULL

Lucky you! Prague is more than just a sightseer's dream; it is a place
to be savoured. With more than a few days here, you can get in all
of the above sights at a leisurely pace, chill out at some funky cafés
or clubs, and take a trip to Karlštejn or Terezín (see pages 126 & 134).

Something for nothing

Prague is a great destination for budget travellers, as the whole city is an open-air museum, accessible 365 days a year, with free admission.

If you enjoy people-watching, the Jan Hus Monument (see page 66), in the middle of the Old Town Square, provides the perfect perch to watch the throngs of tourists. You may even catch some enlightening tour commentary in English from one of the passing groups. An even livelier vantage point is Karlův most (Charles Bridge, see page 94). Here you can hear amusing conversational snippets, cunning pick-up and convincing hard-sell lines, all set to the sound of street musicians and performers. For a bit of loose change, you can stay and watch for as long as you like.

Some beautiful, central spots in Prague are made for rest and relaxation. The gardens leading up to Petřín Hill, the largest of Prague's parks (see page 98), are magical on a hot summer's day and are frequented by frisbee throwers, lovers and only a smattering of tourists. The view from here is enchantingly spire-filled and the clamour of the city is far away.

Prague's hidden churches and cloisters are often used for musical concerts and, therefore, rehearsals. Slip in through the side door, pay your respects, and, if possible, stay for the angelic acoustics.

For museum-goers, the Národní muzeum (National Museum, see page 70) offers visitors free admission on the first Monday of the month. When you pick up the *Prague Post*, check for any gallery exhibition openings. If you dress smartly enough, no one will notice you cruising the wine and buffet table.

There is free Wi-Fi access in many cafés and pubs in the centre of town, though owners do expect you to buy at least something to eat and drink while you're surfing the net.

If you want to feel like a local, feed the swans under Charles Bridge. Or, for a tram's-eye view of Prague, take a window seat on the number 22 as it wends its way around the historical gems of the city. Not quite free, but for 26 Kč you can ride the tram for up to 75 minutes, plenty of time for a circuit of the whole city.

⬥ *Everyone and their dog loves the view from Petřin Hill*

When it rains

Prague's melancholic beauty seems to increase with inclement weather. Rain, sleet or snow shouldn't dampen your spirits, as so many cultural offerings are located indoors, and the reliable public transport system won't keep you waiting for a ride. And, of course, it never rains in pubs and cafés. If you're happy to brave the weather, fortify yourself with a hot grog (rum and hot water with lemon and sugar), grab an umbrella and you'll find that many of the tourist attractions are wonderfully quiet.

A coffee house is always a good choice on a rainy day. Coffee has a firm place in Prague's history; it has been the fuel of Czech literati and dissidents for hundreds of years. The typical Czech coffee house has local newspapers hanging on hooks, a burnished wood interior, lots of cigarette smoke, a crowd of jittery customers, and only one recipe for coffee: *turek*. This Turkish coffee is served in small cups with a thick layer of coffee grounds on the bottom. Then there's the American-inspired bookshop-cum-coffee house, offering frothy lattes, internet access and English literary magazines. Write in your journal, order a steady stream of refreshment, and you can stay as long as you like.

A rainy day is the perfect time to see Josefov, the Jewish Quarter (see page 80), which lends itself to quiet contemplation, or the National Museum (see page 70), with its wonderfully moody corridors filled with prehistoric and anthropological exhibits. Also good on a rainy day is the Prague Castle complex (see page 98), particularly St Vitus Cathedral (see page 100) and the Zlatá ulička (Golden Lane, see page 103), the row of houses where Kafka (patron saint of gloomy weather) lived for a brief stint.

Alternatively, try one of the shopping centres, Palác Flora (see page 119) or Nový Smíchov (see page 106), which offer a variety of diversions under one roof. The former offers an IMAX theatre and 120 fashion shops, and the latter provides not only fashionable shops but a multiplex cinema, food court, athletic gym and the largest games arcade in Prague.

🔺 *Zlatá ulička in the castle precincts*

On arrival

TIME DIFFERENCE
The Czech Republic follows Central European Time, which is one hour ahead of GMT. Daylight Saving applies: clocks go forward by one hour between the end of March and the end of October.

ARRIVING
By air
Prague Airport (☎ 220 113 321 ⓦ www.prg.aero) is 20 km (12 miles) from the city centre and has all the usual airport facilities, including many shops, restaurants and car rental outlets. There are various transport options available. Special airport taxis whisk you to the town centre for upwards of 500 Kč. Pay at the airport taxi information desk in the arrivals hall, and they will issue you a receipt to give to the driver. Alternatively, use the **ČEDAZ minibus service** (☎ 221 111 111 ⓦ www.cedaz.cz) that runs every half-hour between the airport and Naměsti Republiky. Tickets cost 120 Kč (including one piece of luggage; children under ten are free) and are obtained either from the driver or from the booth in the arrivals terminal.

The cheapest way to get into town is by bus. The Airport Express takes you straight to the main Praha Hlavní Nádraží railway station (see opposite), where you can connect to metro line C. Fares are 50 Kč. The local bus number 119 goes to Dejvická metro station, from where it is five stops to the Muzeum metro station in the city centre. The ticket costs 26 Kč from a machine by the bus stop or from the transport information desk in the arrivals terminal (30 Kč if purchased from the driver) and allows you to use Prague's public transport system for up to 75 minutes. You must pay extra for large bags.

IF YOU GET LOST, TRY ...

Excuse me, do you speak English?
Promiňte, mluvíte anglicky?
Prohminyteh, mlooveeteh anglitskee?

**Excuse me, is this the right way to ... the cathedral/
the tourist office/the castle/the old town?**
Promiňte, jedu/jdu správně do ... katedrály/
turistické kanceláře/na hrad/starého města?
*Prohminyteh, yedoo/ydoo sprahvnye doh ... katteddrahlyh/
tooristitskeh kantselahrzeh/na hradd/sterrehoh myestah?*

Can you point to it on my map?
Můžete mi to ukázat na mapě?
Moozheteh mee toh ookahzatt nah mappye?

By rail

Prague has two main railway stations. **Praha Hlavní Nádraží**
(🔵 Wilsonova 8 ☎ 972 241 100; 24-hour info: 840 112 113 🌐 www.vlak.cz)
has a tourist office (🕐 09.00–19.00 Mon–Fri, 09.00–16.00 Sat & Sun)
in the centre of the lower hall. *Úschovna* (luggage storage) is either
coin-operated lockers or a guarded luggage depository. Getting into
the centre of town involves one stop on the metro to the Muzeum
stop, or a walk up busy Wilsonova.

Trains on the main Berlin–Prague–Vienna/Bratislava route call
additionally at the second station, **Praha Holešovice** (🔵 Partyzánská
☎ 840 112 113 Ⓜ Metro: Nádraží Holešovice). The small hall holds the

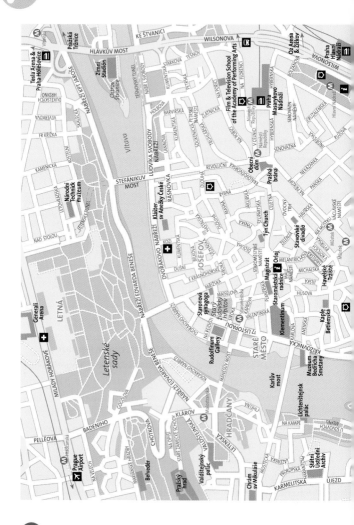

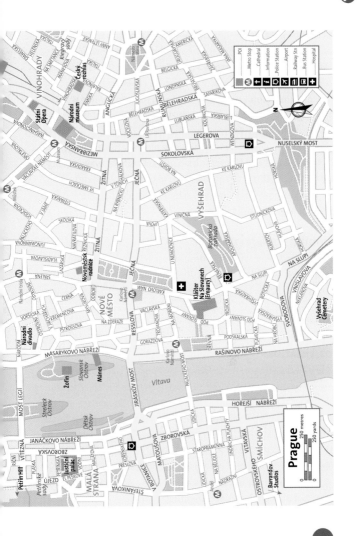

ticket office (🕐 09.00–17.00 Mon–Fri), luggage storage lockers, an internet café and several exchange and accommodation offices (🕐 06.00–23.00). The **Prague Public Transport Co.** has an office here (📞 296 191 817 🌐 www.dpp.cz 🕐 07.00–21.00 Mon–Fri, 09.30–17.00 Sat) and the helpful staff can give you all the information you need to navigate your way around. From Holešovice it is just three stops on the metro to the Muzeum station.

For multilingual, quick and friendly service, avoid the queues at the counters and buy your ticket at the **Czech Railways Agency** (🏢 V Celnici 6 📞 972 233 930 🌐 www.cd.cz 🕐 09.00–17.00).

For up-to-date train and bus schedules in and out of the country, see 🌐 www.vlak-bus.cz.

FINDING YOUR FEET

Prague is a simple city to get around, especially in the centre, which is relatively small and compact. The best way to get the lie of the land is to take the over-ground trams or just walk. The cobblestones and unevenness of the roads call for comfortable footwear; definitely leave the stilettos at home.

ORIENTATION

The Vltava River runs north–south, dividing the city into east and west. The Charles Bridge (see page 94) is the heart of the city, uniting the delights of Staroměstské náměstí (Old Town Square, see page 66), Václavské náměstí (Wenceslas Square, see page 62), Josefov (Jewish Quarter, see page 80) and Nové Město (New Town, see page 60) to the beauty of Malá Strana (Lesser Quarter, see page 94), Petřín Hill (see page 98) and Hradčany (Castle District, see page 94).

Note that building numbers are on blue plaques above the main door, but are not always in consecutive order.

GETTING AROUND

Most of the sights listed in this book are easily (and most enjoyably) accessible on foot, but Prague's efficient, fast and clean public transport system is a good choice if you need to speed across town.

⬥ The tower on Petřín Hill is a useful landmark

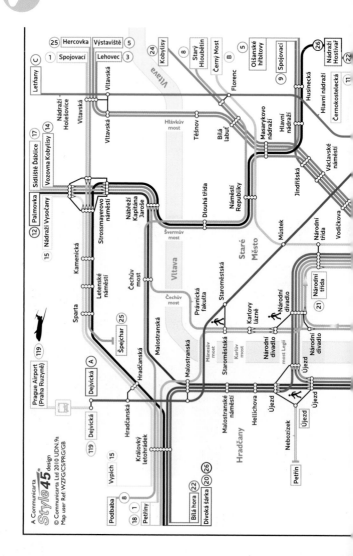

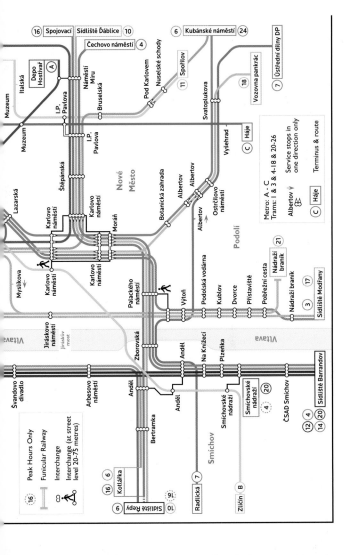

The system, operated by the Prague Public Transport Co. (see page 52), consists of three metro lines, more than twenty tram routes and nine night trams, as well as a network of city buses. The website Ⓦ www.dpp.cz has a good English language section with a journey planner and fare information.

If you plan to use a lot of transport or can't be bothered fiddling about with change and tickets, you can pay 100 Kč for a one-day pass, 330 Kč for a three-day pass or 500 Kč for a five-day pass. Children under six travel free, and the under-15s pay half-price. You will need to buy a 13 Kč ticket for a large backpack or luggage. Remember to validate your ticket by stamping it once at the outset of your journey in the yellow machines at metro entrances and on trams. Failure to do so will earn you a 950 Kč on-the-spot fine from one of the many transport controllers. A controller must show you a gold badge with the metro authority symbol on it as identification. (Some tourists have been conned by fake controllers.)

Muzeum metro station is the junction for the green and red metro lines and is the centre of the Prague metro system. Florenc metro station (pronounced 'Florence') is the junction for the yellow and red lines, and is where the main bus station is located. Hlavní Nádraží metro station is where you will find the main train station.

A crackdown on unscrupulous taxi drivers has resulted in much better control of meters. However, it is always safest to ask your waiter or hotel receptionist to call you a taxi. It costs 40 Kč to step into a taxi, and then a rate of 28 Kč for a kilometre (just over half a mile) or for every two minutes thereafter. **AAA Radiotaxi** (Ⓣ 140 14 or 222 333 222) is one of the best companies.

▶ *Architectural flamboyance on the metro system, too*

CAR HIRE

If you are staying in Prague, it makes no sense to rent a car. If, however, you decide to do a couple of day trips, this is a good option. Most foreign driving licences are valid, including those issued in Canada, the USA and the EU. In the city, the speed limit is 50 km/h (31 miles/h). Outside urban areas it's 90 km/h (56 miles/h), and 130 km/h (81 miles/h) on highways. Seatbelts are compulsory in the front and back seats. You can find rental car agencies directly outside the airport on the ground floor of the airport parking garage and in the city centre.

The following rental companies are generally open on weekdays from 07.00 to 21.00. Many close or have reduced hours at weekends. It makes sense to check out their websites as you can often get better deals online.

A-Rent Car ❶ 224 211 587 Ⓦ www.arentcar.cz

Alimex ❶ 233 350 001 Ⓦ www.alimexcr.cz

Avis ❶ 221 851 225 Ⓦ www.avis.cz

Czechocar CS ❶ 261 222 079 Ⓦ www.czechocar.cz (offering one-way rental to many Czech cities)

Europcar ❶ 224 811 290 Ⓦ www.europcar.cz

Sixt ❶ 222 324 995 Ⓦ www.e-sixt.cz

● *The Powder Tower and the Municipal House, an unlikely coupling*

THE CITY OF
Prague

Staré Město (Old Town) & Nové Město (New Town)

The Old and New Towns of Prague are just that; a combination of old and, well, not quite so old. In Old Town, more than a thousand years of history is captured by its modern visitors as they photograph the beauty of old-world alleyways, baroque balconies and candy-coloured façades. New Town isn't new at all. It was founded in 1348 by Charles IV and is the bustling commercial centre of Prague, blending tradition with innovation, low-end trinket shops with high-end boutiques tucked into art nouveau buildings, all clamouring for your business. Make sure your money belt is secure and your bags zipped, as this is the rip-off route where pickpockets target tourists.

SIGHTS & ATTRACTIONS

Celetná ulice (Celetná Street)

As you follow historic Celetná Street, you are tracing the ancient city walls. Over the centuries, the ground level has sunk by several metres, so examples of the earliest existing architecture in Prague, in all its Romanesque charm, are to be found in the cellars of just about every house along the route. Most houses on this street are either wine bars or restaurants, so you are welcome to duck in for a look. House signs, used to identify Prague houses in the past, are still visible on some buildings on Celetná, such as U bílého páva (At the White Peacock ❸ Celetná 10/557), U černého slunce (At the Black Sun ❸ Celetná 8/556) and U bílého lva (At the White Lion ❸ Celetná 6/555). Along Celetná you'll also find the Ovocný trh (Fruit Market).

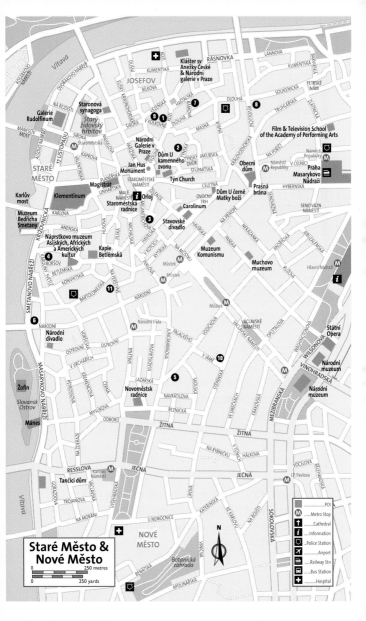

VÁCLAVSKÉ NÁMĚSTÍ (WENCESLAS SQUARE)

In medieval times a horse market, this elongated square is Prague's own Champs-Élysées, dominated at the top of the boulevard by the neo-Renaissance National Museum and surrounded by bars, hotels, shops, cafés, tea houses, restaurants and fast-food stands. To the north of the square is Můstek metro station, where a drawbridge once stood, leading to Old Town. Laid out during the reign of Charles IV, the square lies at the very heart of Prague's New Town, serving as a natural focal point for rallies, protests and parades at key moments in the Czech Republic's history.

In 1969, the 'Prague Spring' saw a young university student, Jan Palach, set himself alight in protest at the Warsaw Pact invasion, while in 1989, during the Velvet Revolution, huge crowds celebrated the fall of Czech Communism as Václav Havel and Alexander Dubček made a historic proclamation from the balcony of the Melantrich building.

From an architectural standpoint there's also plenty to see, with the art nouveau Hotel Evropa, Wiehl House and Peterkův dům all being prime examples of different period styles. At night, dodgy characters and stag-night party-goers take over, leaving you with the choice of joining in or escaping to a quieter part of the city. Ⓜ Metro: Můstek or Muzeum

Dům U černé Matky boží (House of the Black Madonna)

This blocky, eye-catching building is one of the best-known examples of Cubist architecture in Prague, designed by the architect Josef Gočár and built between 1911 and 1912. It houses a permanent

🔺 *Lively Wenceslas Square*

exhibition of Czech Cubism. 🅐 Ovocný trh 19 ☏ 222 310 481
or 224 301 003 🆆 www.ngprague.cz 🕐 10.00–18.00 Tues–Sun
Ⓝ Metro: Nám. Republiky. Admission charge (half price after 16.00)

Klementinum

Covering an area of over 2 hectares (5 acres), this maze of beautiful buildings was built in the early 1700s by the Catholic Church as a college complex devoted to the re-education of the mostly Protestant Bohemians. The most impressive buildings are the magnificent baroque National Library, complete with vast numbers of manuscripts and old books, the lavishly adorned Chapel of Mirrors, where Mozart once played and chamber music concerts are now performed, and the Astronomical Tower, topped with a statue of Atlas. The gallery

◢ Prague's stunning Old Town Square

holds frequently changing exhibitions on various cultural and historical topics. ❸ Křižovnická 190 ❶ 221 663 111 Ⓦ www.nkp.cz ❶ Main hall: 09.00–17.00 Mon–Fri; gallery: 11.00–18.00 Tues–Sun (individual exhibition times may vary) Ⓝ Metro: Staroměstská

Obecní dům (Municipal House)

The Royal Court, where the kings of Bohemia used to stay from the late 14th century onwards, was once located where this art nouveau masterpiece stands today. Built between 1905 and 1910, it has been beautifully restored to its former glory and now holds a Czech and French restaurant, an excellently appointed café, a gallery, shop and classical music venue. This Fabergé egg of architecture was the site for two major Czech events: the declaration of the independent Czechoslovak State was staged in 1918, and, in 1989, the Civic Forum discussed the Velvet transfer of power and the state's transformation into a democratic republic. ❸ Nám. Republiky 5 ❶ 222 002 101 Ⓦ www.obecni-dum.cz ❶ Info centre: 10.00–19.00; tickets: 10.00–18.00 Mon–Fri; enquire for tour times Ⓝ Metro: Nám. Republiky

Prašná brána (Powder Tower)

The Powder Tower was built in 1475 by King Vladislav Jagiello on the site of a 13th-century fortified tower and is an official gateway to the Old Town. Later, it was used to store gunpowder – hence its name. ❸ Na Příkopě, junction with Rybná ❶ 10.00–18.00 Nov–Feb; 10.00–20.00 Mar & Oct; 10.00–22.00 Apr–Sept Ⓝ Metro: Nám. Republiky. Admission charge

Staroměstská radnice (Old Town Hall)

The Old Town Hall is fronted by the Orloj, an astronomical clock that serves as the meeting place in Prague for tourists and locals. As the hour strikes, Jesus and his disciples lead a pageant that includes the allegorical figures of Death, the Turk, the Miser, the Fool and the Proud Rooster. You can also climb (or take the lift) up the tower for stunning views. ⓐ Staroměstské nám. ☏ 724 911 556 ⓛ Tower: 11.00–20.00 Mon, 09.00–20.00 Tues–Sun ⓜ Metro: Staroměstská. Admission charge

Staroměstské náměstí (Old Town Square)

The approach from Celetná to Staroměstské náměstí (Old Town Square) is, in a word, breathtaking. The huge, 1.7 hectare (4 acre) square hosts a hum of activity, day and night, and is usually full of tourists gazing at the pleasing blend of carefully restored Gothic, Renaissance, baroque and neoclassical buildings. A popular activity is to rent a horse and buggy with driver and cruise around town in style, or you can just watch the impromptu musical performances and browse the market stalls. The Old Town Square has a long history as centre stage for so many of the city's defining moments, from the execution of Protestant leaders in 1621 to the attacks on Soviet tanks with Molotov cocktails in 1968. The centrepiece of the square is the Jan Hus Monument, a memorial to the founding father of the Hussite movement.

Towering above the square, half-hidden behind a row of houses, is the fairytale turreted Týn Church. You will notice that the turrets are different; characteristically Gothic, they symbolise male and female elements. Inside the church are late Gothic and baroque altars and the grave of Tycho Brahe, a Danish astronomer who found refuge in the courts of Rudolf II and spent a lot of time debunking the backward planetary beliefs of the Middle Ages by making precise astronomical measurements of the solar system and more than 700 stars. ⓐ Staroměstská

⬥ *Frank Gehry's 'Dancing House' stands out among Prague's historic buildings*

Tančící dům (Dancing House)

Prague's most famous piece of contemporary architecture was built in co-operation with the American architect Frank Gehry on a vacant riverfront plot next to a building owned by Václav Havel, the Czech playwright and former president, whose strong support for avant-garde architecture was instrumental in getting the controversial design approved and built. Locals call the house 'Fred and Ginger', since it vaguely resembles a pair of dancers. The house stands out among the neo-baroque, neo-Gothic and art nouveau buildings for which Prague is famous. Although the building isn't open to the public, there is a highly rated French restaurant, **Celeste** (❶ 221 984 160 Ⓦ www.celesterestaurant.cz ❶ Restaurant: 12.00–14.30, 18.30–22.30 Mon–Sat; bar: 09.00–00.00 Mon–Fri, 10.00–00.00 Sat), on the roof. ❶ Corner of Rasinovo nábř. & Resslova Street ❶ Metro: Karlovo nám.

CULTURE

Dům U kamenného zvonu (Stone Bell House)

The oldest Gothic house in Prague, the Stone Bell House's architectural significance lay hidden to restorers until the 1960s, when they discovered its Gothic origins within the neo-baroque-style building that had been built around it. Today it houses exciting modern art exhibitions run by the City Gallery of Prague. ❶ Staroměstské nám. 13 ❶ 244 827 116 Ⓦ www. ghmp.cz ❶ 10.00–18.00 Tues–Sun ❶ Metro: Staroměstská. Admission charge

Galerie Rudolfinum (Rudolfinum Gallery)

Specialising in modern visual arts, the Rudolfinum is an excellent venue for viewing work from internationally renowned artists as well as emerging local talent. ❶ Alšovo nábř. 12 ❶ 227 059 309

Ⓦ www.galerierudolfinum.cz Ⓛ 10.00–18.00 Tues, Wed, Fri–Sun,
10.00–20.00 Thur Ⓝ Metro: Staroměstská

Muchovo muzeum (Mucha Museum)

This museum is dedicated to perhaps the best-known and most
celebrated Czech art nouveau artist, Alfons Mucha (1860–1939).
Examples of his work are visible all over Prague, particularly at the
Obecní dům (Municipal House) and in the gorgeous stained-glass
windows at St Vitus Cathedral. The exhibits here include Mucha's
paintings, drawings and lithographs as well as his personal belongings.
Ⓐ Kaunický palác, Panská 7 Ⓣ 224 216 415 Ⓦ www.mucha.cz
Ⓛ 10.00–18.00 Ⓝ Metro: Můstek. Admission charge

Muzeum Bedřicha Smetany (Bedrich Smetana Museum)

Housed in a beautiful Renaissance building overlooking the Vltava,
the museum displays letters, music and possessions of famous
Czech composer Smetana – including his earbone. Ⓐ Novotného
lávka 1 Ⓣ 222 220 082 Ⓦ www.nm.cz Ⓛ 10.00–12.00, 12.30–17.00
Wed–Mon Ⓝ Metro: Staroměstská. Admission charge

Muzeum Komunismu (Museum of Communism)

This museum attempts to shed light on the workings of Czechoslovakia's
post-war Communist regime while showing what everyday life was
like for Prague's citizens from 1945 to 1989. The exhibits of propaganda,
censorship and interrogation are striking. The displays of a hotchpotch of
items from school textbooks to border machine guns paint an interesting
picture of the era, leaving you with an eerie feeling of familiarity in
the light of today's war on terror. Ⓐ Na příkopě 10 Ⓣ 224 212 966
Ⓦ www.muzeumkomunismu.cz Ⓛ 09.00–21.00 Ⓝ Metro: Nám.
Republiky or Můstek. Admission charge

Náprstkovo muzeum Asijských, Afrických a Amerických kultur (Náprstek Museum of Asian, African and Native American Culture)

The Náprstek Museum is a branch of the National Museum and contains exhibitions on North African prehistory, ethnography and ancient Egypt, as well as Native American and Inuit culture. Ⓐ Betlémská 1 Ⓣ 224 497 501 Ⓦ www.nm.cz/naprstkovo-muzeum Ⓛ 10.00–18.00 Tues–Sun Ⓝ Metro: Národní třída or Můstek. Admission charge (free 1st Fri of month)

Národní galerie v Praze (National Gallery)

The National Gallery finds its home in many buildings around Prague, and is famous worldwide for its collections. Opening hours for all galleries are 10.00–18.00 Tues–Sun, and Veletržní palác stays open until 21.00 on Thursdays. For information on current exhibitions and events call Ⓣ 222 310 467 or see Ⓦ www.ngprague.cz. Admission charge

Národní muzeum (National Museum)

The National Museum looms at the top of Wenceslas Square, and is worth a visit if only for its sumptuous interior, complete with magnificent double staircases. There is an exhaustive collection of animals, coins, metals, minerals, bones and fossils, many from Bohemia. The museum recently expanded into another historic building at Vinohradská 1. Ⓐ Václavské nám. 68 Ⓣ 224 497 111 Ⓦ www.nm.cz Ⓛ 10.00–17.00; closed 1st Tues of month Ⓝ Metro: Muzeum. Admission charge (free 1st Mon of month)

Stavovské divadlo (Estates Theatre)

This is Prague's oldest theatre, which staged the world premiere of Mozart's opera, *Don Giovanni*, in 1787. Not far from here stands the Carolinum, once a college of Charles University founded by Charles IV, comprising several buildings in the Gothic style. ⓐ Ovocný trh 1 ❶ 224 901 448 Ⓦ www.narodni-divadlo.cz ❶ Box office: 10.00–18.00 & 45 mins before show; tours can be booked at PIS office (see page 151) Ⓝ Metro: Můstek

RETAIL THERAPY

Černá růže A modern shopping centre on Na příkopě containing a mix of shops, cafés and restaurants. Outlets include Adidas, Bang & Olufsen, Daniel Hechter, Dolce & Gabbana and Mambo. ⓐ Na příkopě 12 ❶ 221 014 111 Ⓦ www.cernaruze.cz ❶ 09.00–20.00 Mon–Fri, 09.00–19.00 Sat, 11.00–19.00 Sun Ⓝ Metro: Můstek

Dr Stuart's Botanicus With prime locations in Prague, this chain of natural scent, soap and herb shops is an amazing Anglo-Czech success story. Started by a British botanist and Czech partner on a farm northeast of Prague, Dr Stuart's create sumptuously scented products that make great gifts to take back home. ⓐ Týnský dvůr (behind Týn Church) / Michalská 4, next to Havelské Tržiště ❶ 234 767 446 Ⓦ www.botanicus.cz ❶ 10.00–20.00 Ⓝ Metro: Staroměstská or Můstek

Dům hudebních nástrojů This music shop stocks everything from drum kits and bagpipes to pianos and penny whistles. Many of the instruments are made in the Czech Republic, making this a great place for both musicians and memento hunters to explore. ⓐ Jungmannovo nám. 17 ❶ 224 236 303 Ⓦ www.dhn.cz ❶ 09.00–18.00 Mon–Fri, 10.00–14.00 Sat Ⓝ Metro: Můstek or Národní třída

Dům módy A giant fashion store for men, women and children – the place to come if you want cool clothes in a hurry. ⓐ Václavské nám. 58 ❶ 234 101 904 Ⓦ www.d-mody.cz ⓛ 09.00–20.00 Mon–Fri, 10.00–20.00 Sat, 10.00–19.00 Sun Ⓝ Metro: Můstek

Havelské tržiště Havel's Market is Prague's best open-air market, with fine examples of art, ceramics, leather goods, woodwork, and even a good selection of food items. Give yourself time to browse the stalls. ⓐ Havelská ul. 13 ❶ 602 340 299 ⓛ 07.00–18.30 Jan–Mar; 07.00–19.30 Apr–Dec Ⓝ Metro: Můstek

Lahůdky zemark This typical Czech deli on Wenceslas Square has been serving Czech and Moravian wines and spirits, mayonnaise-drenched salads, sticks of the finest salami and lots of other Bohemian goodies for as long as anyone can remember. ⓐ Václavské nám. 42 ❶ 224 210 034 ⓛ 07.00–19.30 Mon–Fri, 07.00–18.00 Sat Ⓝ Metro: Můstek or Muzeum

Manufaktura Features unique handicrafts, wooden toys and hand-made skincare products. Their home-spun linens are unique. Many locations around town, but the main one is at ⓐ Melantrichova 17 ❶ 221 632 480 Ⓦ www.manufaktura.biz ⓛ 10.00–19.30 Sun–Thur, 10.00–20.00 Fri & Sat Ⓝ Metro: Můstek

Modernista If you're interested in Czech art and design, come straight here. There's a good selection of ceramics as well as art deco or cubist-inspired furniture. ⓐ Celetná 12 ❶ 224 241 200 Ⓦ www.modernista.cz ⓛ 11.00–19.00 Ⓝ Metro: Nám. Republiky

Myslbek This shopping centre is probably the most lavish and well-equipped in Prague, with a good range of shops such as

Marlboro Classics, H&M, Calvin Klein, Gant USA and Next, to name a few. There's also a sushi bar. ⓐ Na příkopě 19/21 ⓣ 224 239 550 ⓦ www.ngmyslbek.cz ⓒ Centre: 08.00–22.00; shops: 09.00–20.00 Mon–Sat, 10.00–19.00 Sun ⓝ Metro: Můstek

Palladium Behind a beautifully renovated historical façade lies Prague's most central temple to consumer choice. Where once there was just a derelict barracks now rise five glittering floors packed with 170 of your favourite brand names, 30 eateries and the largest car park in central Prague. ⓐ Nám. Republiky 1 ⓣ 225 770 250 ⓦ www.palladiumpraha.cz ⓒ 09.00–21.00 Sun–Wed, 09.00–22.00 Thur–Sat ⓝ Metro: Nám. Republiky

Promod A favourite with the uptown crowd, this unique French clothing store for women has some excellent bargains on the second floor. ⓐ Václavské nám. 2 ⓣ 296 327 701 ⓦ www.promod.eu ⓒ 09.00–21.00 ⓝ Metro: Můstek

RPM: Tamizdat Record Shop Revolutionise your music selection in this incredible shop that focuses on Central and Eastern European indies. It is situated in the Unijazz organisation café (head up courtyard stairway number 2 to the fourth floor), where you can have a cup of coffee or beer while listening to their eclectic mix. ⓐ Jindřišská 5 ⓣ 222 240 934 ⓦ www.tamizdat.org ⓒ 14.00–22.00 Mon–Thur, 14.00–21.00 Fri ⓝ Metro: Můstek

Slovanský dům With a prestigious address on Na příkopě, this large complex offers a range of swish shops and boutiques as well as places to eat, drink and relax (read: Thai massage parlour). For movie-goers there's also a state-of-the-art Star City

multiplex within the centre. ⓐ Na příkopě 22 ⓣ 221 451 400
ⓦ www.slovanskydum.com ⓛ 10.00–20.00 ⓜ Metro: Můstek

TAKING A BREAK

Even in the heat of the tourist season, there are enclaves of quiet
within the heart of Old Town, where you can grab a good coffee,
a light snack, and relax. Some of Prague's newest eateries cater to
the veggie crowd and are refreshingly inexpensive and wholesome
– a good foil for the damage done to livers in the evening hours.

Bakeshop Praha £ ❶ This bakery is the absolute best in Prague for
cakes, croissants, quiches, and quick customer service. It is mainly
a take-away affair, with a few strategically placed stools overlooking
the street. Try the *focaccia* bread sandwiches and chocolate brownies.
ⓐ Kozi 1 ⓣ 222 316 823 ⓦ www.bakeshop.cz ⓛ 07.00–19.00
ⓜ Metro: Nám. Republiky, then tram: 5, 8, 14 to Dlouhá třída

Beas Vegetarian Dhaba £ ❷ This Indian vegetarian eatery is popular
with locals and tourists alike. Maybe it's the sunny atmosphere,
the huge portions and the reasonable prices that keep them coming
back for more. ⓐ Týnská 19 ⓣ 608 035 727 ⓦ www.beas-dhaba.cz
ⓛ 11.00–20.00 Mon–Sat, 11.00–18.00 Sun ⓜ Metro: Staroměstská

Country Life £ ❸ Prague's foremost veggie haven, Country Life
is often crowded at lunchtime, but if you go earlier or later
you're sure to find a seat at the cafeteria-style counter. Even
non-vegetarians are impressed with the great salads, pizzas and
hearty soups, and there's a shop inside where you can stock up for
picnics. ⓐ Melantrichova 15 ⓣ 224 213 366 ⓦ www.countrylife.cz

MAITREA vege.

🕐 08.30–19.00 Mon–Thur, 08.30–18.00 Fri, 11.00–18.00 Sun (closes early Fri in winter) Ⓜ Metro: Můstek

Lehká Hlava £ ❹ This restaurant, just a short walk from Charles Bridge, blends a décor of Asia-inspired motifs and Eastern religious iconography with an international meat-free and vegan menu in a smoke-free environment. A well-designed eatery with fab food and

🔺 *Relax with a coffee under the arches of the Old Town Square*

a relaxed ambience. ⓐ Boršov 2 ❶ 222 220 665 Ⓦ www.lehkahlava.cz
🕐 11.30–23.30 Mon–Fri, 12.00–23.30 Sat & Sun Ⓝ Tram: 17 & 18 to
Karlovy lázně

Novoměstský Pivovar (New Town Brewery) ££ ❺ This is one of Prague's
microbreweries, producing its own light and dark beers. If you are an
early riser, you can sample a brew over a hearty breakfast; if not, have
a beer or two over lunch at the pleasant brewery restaurant. It offers
a full range of traditional beer-hall food, and the chance to order a
whole suckling pig for large groups. ⓐ Vodičkova ul. 20 ❶ 222 232 448
Ⓦ www.npivovar.cz 🕐 10.00–23.30 Mon–Fri, 11.30–23.30 Sat,
12.00–22.00 Sun Ⓝ Metro: Můstek

Slavia ££ ❻ A swish 1930s interior, scurrying waiters, the tinkle
of glasses and coffee cups and the gentle hubbub of highbrow
conversation make this Bohemian institution an essential Prague
experience. ⓐ Smetanovo nábř. 2 ❶ 224 218 493 Ⓦ www.cafeslavia.cz
🕐 08.00–00.00 Mon–Fri, 09.00–00.00 Sat & Sun Ⓝ Metro:
Národní třída

AFTER DARK

RESTAURANTS
Ariana £ ❼ Afghan rugs, water pipes, Eastern tones emitting from
the CD player and large portions of rice, kebabs and salad make the
capital's only Afghan restaurant an Oriental oasis of relaxation and
an exotic refuelling stop in the heart of the Old Town. ⓐ Rámová 6
❶ 222 323 438 Ⓦ www.kabulrest.sweb.cz 🕐 11.00–23.00 Ⓝ Metro:
Nám. Republiky

Dahab ££ ❽ A combination of tea room, patisserie, café and restaurant, the Dahab offers a range of Middle-Eastern dishes, including vegetarian options, plus *hookahs* (water pipes) to puff on. Belly dancers really get things going on Thursday, Friday and Saturday nights from 21.30. ⓐ Soukenická 4 ❶ 222 317 732 Ⓦ www.dahab.cz Ⓛ 11.00–01.00 Mon–Fri, 14.00–03.00 Sat, 14.00–00.00 Sun Ⓝ Metro: Nám Republiky or Staroměstská

Kolkovna ££ ❾ This Czech chain restaurant in the centre of town has Pilsner on tap and a beer garden out the back. ⓐ V Kolkovně 8 ❶ 224 819 701 Ⓦ www.kolkovna.cz Ⓛ 10.00–00.00 Ⓝ Metro: Staroměstská

Restaurace Jáma ££ ❿ Inside this fast-paced American and Tex-Mex eatery, you'll find the waiting staff offering friendly service and the best burgers in town. ⓐ V jámě 7 ❶ 224 222 383 Ⓦ www.jamapub.cz Ⓛ 11.00–01.00 Ⓝ Metro: Můstek

Restaurace U mědvídku ££ ⓫ Serves great Bohemian grub, with Budvar on tap and a busy, beer-hall vibe. ⓐ Na Perštýně 7 ❶ 224 211 916 Ⓦ www.umedvidku.cz Ⓛ 11.30–23.00 Ⓝ Metro: Národní třída

BARS, CLUBS & THEATRES

Divadlo Archa One of the best-equipped, mid-sized alternative theatre venues in Europe, featuring interactive shows that utilise technology, dance and puppetry. If you buy your tickets early, you can chill out before the show at the theatre café next door. ⓐ Na Poříčí 26 ❶ 221 716 333 Ⓦ www.archatheatre.cz Ⓛ Box office: 10.00–18.00 & 2 hrs before start of performance Ⓝ Metro: Florenc or Nám. Republiky

Duplex A venue offering a combination of nightclub, café and restaurant, Duplex tends to stick to resident DJs. The outdoor terrace offers a view overlooking the sights of Wenceslas Square. Ⓐ Václavské nám. 21 Ⓣ 732 221 111 Ⓦ www.duplex.cz Ⓝ Metro: Můstek

Laterna Magika (Magic Lantern) Visually stunning multimedia techniques combine with film and contemporary dance to convey intriguing and imaginative ideas. Housed in Nová Scéna (part of the National Theatre, see below). Ⓐ Ostrovní 1 Ⓣ 224 931 482 Ⓦ www.laterna.cz Ⓝ Metro: Národní třída

Národní divadlo (National Theatre) This lavish neo-Renaissance building on the bank of the Vltava, with its golden crown of chariot-driving women, is a Czech cultural institution. Three artistic ensembles — opera, ballet and drama — alternate performances in the historic building of the National Theatre, in the Stavovské divadlo (Estates Theatre) and in the Kolowrat Theatre. Ⓐ Ostrovní 1 Ⓣ 224 901 448 Ⓦ www.nationaltheatre.cz Ⓝ Metro: Národní třída

Reduta Jazz Club Prague's top jazz venue, where Bill Clinton gave his famous saxophone performance in 1994. Ⓐ Národní třída 20 Ⓣ 224 933 487 Ⓦ www.redutajazzclub.cz Ⓛ 21.00–late Ⓝ Metro: Národní třída

Roxy An authentically underground gutted art deco building that continues to be one of the best clubs in town. Funk and techno DJs spin this place into a frothed-up frolic pad. Arrive around midnight, when the fun begins. Ⓐ Dlouhá 33 Ⓣ 602 691 015 Ⓦ www.roxy.cz Ⓛ 19.00–00.00 Mon–Thur, 19.00–06.00 Fri–Sun Ⓝ Metro: Nám. Republiky

U zlatého tygra (The Golden Tiger) Central Prague's most down-to-earth pub, where the grub's filling and the beer's cheap and good. Tightly packed benches mean you very soon learn everything you didn't want to about your fellow drinkers. ⓐ Husova 17 ⓣ 222 221 111 ⓦ www.uzlatehotygra.cz ⓛ 15.00–23.00 ⓝ Metro: Staroměstská

🔺 *Prague's National Theatre is right on the bank of the Vltava River*

Josefov (Jewish Quarter)

The site of the oldest Jewish settlement in Europe is Prague's haunting historic Jewish Quarter, Josefov, nestled in winding side streets off Maiselova ul., north of the Old Town Square. It is a place where Prague's dark past collides with its fashionable future – where you can almost hear the buildings sinking deeper into their foundations, while decadent culinary and fashion pursuits beckon the visitor to the hidden streets and back alleys. It is absolutely most profitably explored on foot.

Named after Emperor Josef II, whose reforms helped to ease living conditions for the Jews, Josefov was once a walled-in area and now holds the historic remains of what used to be a populous ghetto. Only six synagogues, the Ceremonial Hall, the Town Hall and the Old Jewish Cemetery were left standing when the old Jewish buildings were torn down due to neglect, disease and infestation.

CULTURE

Klausová synagoga (Klausen Synagogue)

Rising from the ashes of the fire that devastated Josefov in 1689, Klausen Synagogue was rebuilt in 1694. The largest of the six synagogues in the Jewish ghetto, Klausen was the home of the Jewish Burial Society in Prague. A permanent exhibit, entitled *Jewish Customs and Traditions*, shows everyday life in the Jewish community and customs connected with birth, circumcision, bar mitzvah, weddings, divorce and the Jewish household. The second half of this exhibit is located in the Ceremonial Hall next door.

ⓐ U Starého hřbitova 1 🕐 09.00–18.00 Sun–Fri, summer; 09.00–16.30 Sun–Fri, winter

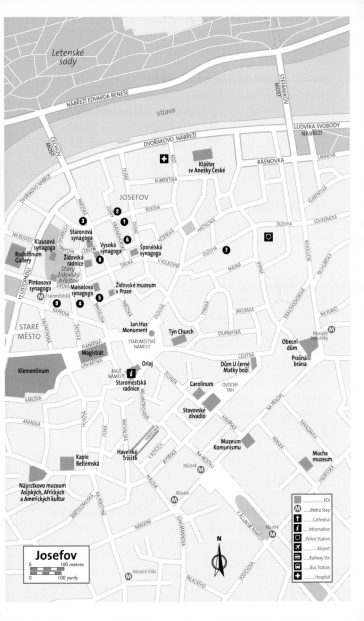

Maiselova synagoga (Maisel Synagogue)

Housing a fascinating collection of Jewish silver, textiles, prints and books, most of them brought to Prague by the Nazis, Maisel Synagogue is named after Mordechai Maisel, the mayor of Prague's Jewish Quarter, who funded the extensive Renaissance reconstruction of the ghetto. It is currently used as an exhibition venue and depository. ❸ Maiselova 10 🕐 09.00–18.00 Sun–Fri, summer; 09.00–16.30 Sun–Fri, winter

Pinkasova synagoga (Pinkas Synagogue)

Founded in 1479, Pinkas Synagogue was first turned into a memorial to the Czech Holocaust victims in 1958. Ten years later, the Communist government closed the memorial and removed the names from the wall. The names were rewritten on the wall after the fall of Communism in 1989. There is a collection here of paintings and drawings done by children held at the Terezín concentration camp in North Bohemia during World War II. ❸ Široká 3 🕐 09.00–18.00 Sun–Fri, summer; 09.00–16.30 Sun–Fri, winter

Španělská synagoga (Spanish Synagogue)

This neo-Moorish structure was built in 1868. It is a beautiful building inside and out, with a domed ceiling, Islamic motifs and stained glass. There is an exhibition on the history of Czech Jews. ❸ Dušní 12 🕐 09.00–18.00 Sun–Fri, summer; 09.00–16.30 Sun–Fri, winter

Staronová synagoga (Old-New Synagogue)

Of all the synagogues in Prague, this is perhaps the most important. It has stood here since the 13th century, and despite fires, floods and the Nazi occupation, it remains the functional, spiritual centre of the Jewish community. Built around 1270 by Christian architects (as Jews could not be architects), the Old-New Synagogue is the oldest working synagogue in Europe and one of Prague's earliest Gothic buildings. As in all Orthodox synagogues, the men and women are segregated and only the men are allowed in the main hall. This is a single-storey building, so the women's galley is not upstairs, as is customary. Instead, there are side corridors where the women stand to view the services through narrow slits in the wall. Franz Kafka's bar mitzvah was held here. ⓐ Červená 2 ⓦ www.synagogue.cz ⓛ 09.30–17.00 Sun–Fri, Nov–Mar; 09.30–18.00 Sun–Fri, Apr–Oct. Admission charge

Starý židovský hřbitov (Old Jewish Cemetery)

One of the most impressive sights in the Jewish Quarter is the Old Jewish Cemetery. It was used from 1439 to 1787 and is the oldest existing Jewish cemetery in Europe. The Nazis made it a policy to destroy Jewish cemeteries, sometimes using the tombstones for target practice, but Hitler ordered that this one be left intact.

● *Josefov's Old Jewish Cemetery is an atmospheric and beautiful place*

There are more than 100,000 Jews buried in this small plot; the graves are layered 12-deep in some places. The graves stand crowded and askew, decorated with small pebbles placed by visitors, as is the custom. The most prominent graves are those of Mordechai Maisel, a leader of the Prague Jewish community in the 1600s, and Rabbi Loew, the mystical Rabbi who summoned forth the Golem (see page 88). ⓐ Široká 2, entrance from Pinkas Synagogue 🕐 11.00–15.00 Mon & Wed, 09.00–13.00 Fri. Admission charge

Vysoká synagoga (High Synagogue)
Founded by Mordechai Maisel, the mayor of Prague's Jewish Quarter, the High Synagogue is no longer open to the public for tours. It was named for the lofty position of its prayer room located on the second floor of the building. It now functions as a non-Orthodox synagogue. ⓐ Červená 4

Židovská radnice (Jewish Town Hall)
An 18th-century Rococo building, the Jewish Town Hall is the centre of Prague's Jewish community today. Note the clock on the façade with Hebrew numbers; the hands turn counter-clockwise, because Hebrew reads from right to left. ⓐ Maiselova 18

CULTURE

Židovské muzeum v Praze (Jewish Museum of Prague)
Founded in 1906 in order to preserve artefacts from the demolition of the many Josefov buildings, the Jewish Museum now houses one of the most extensive collections of Jewish art, textiles and silver in the world. The Nazis closed the museum soon after their occupation of Prague, using the building to hold all the objects they had

◆ *Jewish Museum of Prague*

confiscated from the synagogues in Bohemia and Moravia. During World War II, Jewish artefacts from all over Europe were brought to Prague and stored in preparation for the museum that Hitler planned to build on this site, 'The Exotic Museum of an Extinct Race'. The entrance fee for the Jewish Museum gives you access to six other historic sites – the Klausen, Maisel, Pinkas and Spanish synagogues, the Old Jewish Cemetery and the Ceremonial Hall – and the Robert Gutmann Gallery. The ticket can be bought at any one of these sites. Men are required to cover their heads with the paper hats provided. Women do not need to wear any type of head cover. ⓐ U Staré školy 1 ① 221 711 511 ⓦ www.jewishmuseum.cz ⓛ 09.00–18.00 Sun–Fri, summer; 09.00–16.30 Sun–Fri, winter. Admission charge

RETAIL THERAPY

Pařížská, named after the city of Paris, is the Jewish Quarter's main thoroughfare and is now the swankiest shopping section in town, being home to Louis Vuitton, Hermès, Francesca Biasia, and the Czech home accessories store, Le Patio. The nearby streets Dlouhá, Dušní and V Kolkovně are emerging as a fashion district, attracting some of the country's best-known designers, including Bohéme, Klára Nademlýnská, Tatiana and Timoure et Group. All these shops are close to the Staroměstská metro station.

Bohēme An affordable, modern Czech clothing store for women, with particularly good sweaters and leather jackets. ⓐ Dušní 8 ① 224 813 840 ⓦ www.boheme.cz ⓛ 11.00–19.00 Mon–Fri, 11.00–17.00 Sat

◆ *Strolling around the Jewish Quarter*

THE GOLEM

Throughout Prague you may see items with the word 'Golem' on them. These relate to Jewish Prague's version of the Frankenstein monster. Golem originally meant 'embryo' or 'imperfect matter', though it is now a Hebrew and Yiddish slang term for a person not thought to be intellectually eminent.

The story begins during the reign of Emperor Rudolf II in the 17th century. The emperor was indifferent to the church, and entertained alchemists, artists, astronomers and mystics at court. He befriended Rabbi Loew, a well-known Jewish scholar and expert in interpreting the Cabbala. Rabbi Loew became a favoured 'Court Jew', frequently able to intercede on behalf of Jews who were being routinely persecuted at that time.

As alchemists try to make gold out of base metals, cabbalists work on ways of animating simple matter. Rabbi Loew, so the story goes, took a ball of clay from the Vltava River, formed a figure out of it, placed in its mouth a *shem*, or charm, and the Golem came to life. The Rabbi ordered the Golem to protect the Jewish Quarter from attack. But the monster had a mind of its own.

Legend has it that the Golem finally ran amok and the Rabbi had to interrupt his Sabbath service in the synagogue to deal with it. His congregation kept repeating the verse in a psalm that they had been reciting until the Rabbi returned. To commemorate this event, a line repeats in the Sabbath service at the Old-New Synagogue to this day. The end of the Golem came when the Rabbi removed the *shem* from its mouth and carried its lifeless remains to the attic of the Old-New Synagogue where they allegedly reside to this day.

🔺 *Take home a souvenir Golem*

Chez Parisienne Gives you a glimpse of what the high-powered executives and local diplomats wear under their outers. ⓐ Pařížská 8 ⓣ 224 814 593 🕙 10.00–19.00 Mon–Sat, 12.00–19.00 Sun

Fabergé Once jewellers to the Romanovs, Fabergé is still the last word in elegance. Trademark egg pendants and other glittering creations can be found at the Prague branch, which ominously has no prices displayed in its shop windows. ⓐ Pařížská 15 ⓣ 222 323 639 🕙 10.00–20.00

Francesco Biasia She's known for her fur purses and buttery leather goods. Storekeepers boast that their business is 90 per cent Czech, which ensures that what you buy will be a unique piece back home. ⓐ Pařížská 24 ⓣ 224 815 846 ⓦ www.biasia.it ⓛ 10.30–19.30 Mon–Fri, 11.00–19.30 Sat, 12.00–19.00 Sun

Hermès Stocking a colourful array of iconic ties and scarves, there are also a few other fashion gems that break away from the typical Hermès line. ⓐ Pařížská 12 ⓣ 224 817 545 ⓦ www.hermes.com ⓛ 10.00–19.00 Mon–Fri, 10.00–18.00 Sat, 12.00–18.00 Sun

Klára Nademlýnská One of the Czech Republic's best-known young designers, Klára ensures hot haute fashion in the best-looking boutique in town. ⓐ Dlouhá 3 ⓣ 224 818 769 ⓦ www.klaranademlynska.cz ⓛ 10.00–19.00 Mon–Fri, 10.00–18.00 Sat

Louis Vuitton This Prague shop stocks the full line of trademark beige-and-brown LV handbags and other luxurious accessories. ⓐ Pařížská 13 ⓣ 224 812 774 ⓦ www.louisvuitton.com ⓛ 10.00–19.00 Mon–Fri, 10.00–18.00 Sat, 12.00–18.00 Sun

Tatiana Tatiana Kovaříková creates beautiful women's clothes. It's definitely worth poking around this shop to see what's on offer, from corsets to zip-up capes. ⓐ Dušní 1 ⓣ 224 813 723 ⓦ www.tatiana.cz ⓛ 10.00–19.00 Mon–Fri, 11.00–16.00 Sat

Timoure et Group A pair of Czech designers who create well-tailored coats, suits, trousers, jackets and sweaters, with a dash of inspiration. ⓐ V Kolkovně 6 ⓣ 222 327 358 ⓦ www.timoure.cz ⓛ 10.00–19.00 Mon–Fri, 11.00–17.00 Sat

TAKING A BREAK

Bakery Mansson £ ❶ This bakery is so good, they baked the cake for Mick Jagger's 60th birthday party celebration. Simple interior, with only a few café tables and a long counter that boasts a delicious selection of breads and cakes. Healthy breakfasts are served, and lunches mean homemade rye bread sandwiches stuffed with all kinds of fillings, and there are salads, too. ❸ Bílkova 8 ❶ 222 310 620 🕐 07.00–19.00 Mon–Fri, 08.00–19.00 Sat & Sun ⓝ Metro: Staroměstská or Nám. Republiky

Potrefená husa £ ❷ This is part of a modern, brewery-owned chain. Their menu is straightforward, the beer is tasty and service is usually very good (sadly uncommon in these parts). ❸ Bílkova 5 ❶ 222 326 626 ⓦ www.potrefenahusa.com 🕐 11.00–00.00 ⓝ Metro: Staroměstská, then tram: 17 or 53 to Právnická fakulta

Reduta £ ❸ A window-wrapped Continental café that's a good place for lunch or an afternoon drink. The restaurant is perfect in warm weather, when rattan chairs and tables tumble onto the pavement. The steaks are excellent. ❸ Pařížská 19 ❶ 222 327 260 🕐 09.00–00.00 ⓝ Metro: Staroměstská

Restaurace v Žatecké £ ❹ This unpretentious oasis of down-to-earth Czech hospitality in increasingly gentrified Josefov serves up cheap filling lunches and Pilsner beer in a simple cellar dining space. The goulash and roast duck with dumplings and red cabbage are Bohemian comfort foods at their tastiest. ❸ Žatecká 10 ❶ 224 819 155 🕐 11.00–23.00 ⓝ Metro: Staroměstská

AFTER DARK

RESTAURANTS

U Golema £ Dark furniture, walls and ceiling and even monstrous service all seem to be in keeping with the Golem theme. Local and international dishes are on offer as well as excellent Moravian wines. ⓐ Maiselova 8 ⓣ 222 328 165 ⓦ www.restaurantugolema.cz ⓛ 10.00–23.30 ⓝ Metro: Staroměstská

Café La Veranda ££ Offers 'fusion light' specialities in a modern setting. For a special occasion, try the 'sexy menu', a combination of five of the best *entrées*. ⓐ Elišky Krásnohorské 2/10 ⓣ 224 814 733 ⓦ www.laveranda.cz ⓛ 12.00–00.00 Mon–Sat ⓝ Metro: Staroměstská

Láry Fáry ££ Design-heavy place with good sound, excellent location and an extensive menu of dishes. Try the skewered meats. Good first-date pick. ⓐ Dlouhá 30 ⓣ 222 320 154 ⓦ www.laryfary.cz ⓛ 11.00–00.00 ⓝ Metro: Nám. Republiky

Restaurace Pravda ££ Situated beside the Old-New Synagogue, this stylish space offers risky global fusion and caters to vegetarians and meat-eaters alike. Cool lighting, comfortable seating and helpful staff. ⓐ Pařížská 17 ⓣ 222 326 203 ⓦ www.pravdarestaurant.cz ⓛ 12.00–01.00 ⓝ Metro: Staroměstská

La Bodeguita del Medio ££–£££ Always packed, this upmarket Cuban restaurant offers live music, a cigar lounge and a cocktail bar as well as excellent seafood and Latin American specialities.

Ⓐ Kaprova 5 ❶ 224 813 922 Ⓦ www.bodeguita.cz ◷ 09.00–02.00
Ⓝ Metro: Staroměstská

BARS, CLUBS & THEATRES

Aloha Wave Lounge Cool fun in summer and a hot spot in winter.
A wood interior and dimmed lights provide a relaxed ambience
while you watch surfing films on the wide screen, sip exotic
cocktails or toss back some Pacific cuisine. Live DJs and bands play
regularly. Ⓐ Dušní 11 ❶ 602 251 392 ◷ Cafe: 09.30–02.00 Sun–Tues,
09.30–04.00 Wed–Sat; cocktail lounge: 18.00–02.00 Sun–Tues,
18.00–04.00 Wed–Sat Ⓝ Metro: Staroměstská

Karma Lounge Excellent Lebanese restaurant by day, exotic dance
club by night with belly dancing, salsa and reggae nights as well as
a disco with live music every Saturday. Ⓐ Klimentská 4 ❶ 774 143 043
Ⓦ www.karmalounge.cz ◷ 14.00–23.00 Mon & Tues, 15.00–late
Wed & Thur, 17.00–late Fri & Sat Ⓝ Metro: Staroměstská

NoD No, nobody sleeps here. NoD is a multifunctional space in
the centre of Prague which contains a theatre, gallery, media lab,
cinema, presentation hall and café. Ⓐ Above the Roxy on Dlouhá 33
❶ 224 826 330 Ⓦ www.roxy.cz ◷ 14.00–22.00 Ⓝ Metro: Nám.
Republiky, then tram: 8 or 14 to Dlouhá třída

Malá Strana (Lesser Quarter) & Hradčany

Hradčany is where Prague Castle lords over Prague. The ascent on foot, tram or metro provides you with many sublime views of the city, its grandeur laid out before you in all directions. The clifftop site is certainly fit for a monarch, and the castle complex itself is rich in architectural gems.

The Malá Strana (Lesser Quarter) is anything but diminutive. This storybook-beautiful area was founded in the 13th century by merchants who set up shop at the base of the castle. Traced with narrow, winding lanes boasting palaces and red-roofed burgher houses, Malá Strana is filled with pricier pubs and restaurants, quirky boutiques and foreign embassies. If you feel a sense of déjà vu, it's because the area has played a prominent part in many Czech and foreign films.

SIGHTS & ATTRACTIONS

Chrám sv. Mikuláše (St Nicholas Church)

This church is one of the most valuable buildings of the Prague baroque period, complete with dominant dome and belfry. The inside decoration of the church is a glorious example of high baroque style. Mozart played the organ here during his stay in Prague. The church is often used as a concert venue.❸ Malostranské nám. 25 ❶ 224 190 991 ❺ Visits: 09.00–16.00; concerts: usually 17.00 Ⓜ Metro: Malostranská. Admission charge

Karlův most (Charles Bridge)

Dating from 1357, one of Prague's foremost attractions links Prague Castle and the Malá Strana to Staré Město. Built to replace the earlier,

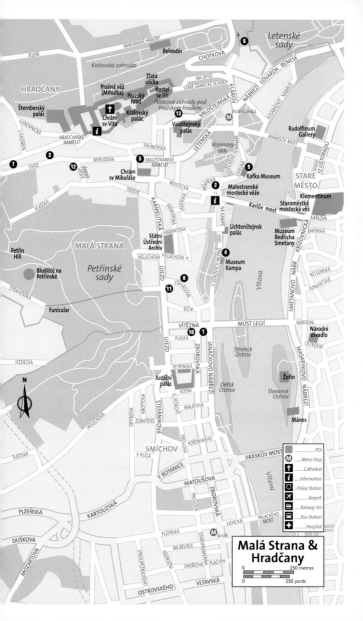

Malá Strana & Hradčany

0	250 metres
0	250 yards

Legend:
- POI
- Ⓜ Metro Stop
- ✝ Cathedral
- ⓘ Information
- 🏛 Police Station
- ✈ Airport
- 🚆 Railway Stn
- 🚌 Bus Station
- ✚ Hospital

12th-century Judith's Bridge, this 500 m (¹/₃ mile) span has survived floods and acted as Prague's main pedestrian promenade across the Vltava River for nearly 600 years. Today, the bridge hosts a busy mix of tourists, locals, artists and busking minstrels. The best time to stroll across the bridge is early morning and around sunset, when the crowds have thinned and lamplight casts mysterious shadows on the 30 hulking statues along its edge. The oldest of these portrays Jan of Nepomuk, one of the most popular Bohemian saints, supposedly martyred by King Wenceslas for refusing to divulge the confessional secrets of the king's wife, who was cheating on her husband. The newest of the statues depicts Cyril and Methodius, brothers born in the Byzantine Empire in the ninth century who became Christian missionaries to the Slavic peoples. The statues are all copies, the valuable originals being housed in the Lapidarium of the National Gallery (see page 70).

Malostranské mostecké věže (Lesser Town Bridge Towers)

Located at the western end of Charles Bridge, the smaller tower is the remaining relic of Judith Bridge, a Romanesque bridge constructed in the 12th century and destroyed by flood in 1342. The taller tower was designed to match the Old Town Bridge Tower. The permanent exhibition within this tower on the history of Charles Bridge is worth a visit. ❶ 257 530 487 ❼ www.prazskeveze.cz ❸ 10.00–22.00 Apr–Sept; 10.00–21.00 Oct & Mar; 10.00–18.00 Nov–Feb ❾ Metro: Malostranská. Admission charge

Palácové zahrady pod Pražským hradem (Palatial Gardens below Prague Castle)

Situated on the southern slopes of the castle you'll find beautiful views of Malá Strana among the fussy terraces, monumental staircases and fountains of these truly palatial gardens.

◔ *Inspirational views on Charles Bridge*

ⓐ Valdštejnské nám. 3 ⓣ 257 010 401 ⓦ www.palacovezahrady.cz
ⓛ 10.00–17.00 Mar; 10.00–18.00 Apr & Oct; 10.00–19.00 May & Sept;
10.00–21.00 June & July; 10.00–20.00 Aug ⓝ Metro: Malostranská.
Admission charge

Petřín Hill

Ride the funicular to the top of this hill to find a miniature Eiffel
Tower that functioned as the city's primary telecommunications
tower until the Žižkov TV Tower opened across town. Those who
climb the 59 m (195 ft) tower will be treated to striking views, day or
night. Just hanging around in the gardens is fun. Bring a frisbee and
a picnic, and make an afternoon of it. Another enjoyable diversion
is the Bludiště na Petříně, a mirror maze with a depiction of Prague
students fighting against Swedes on the Charles Bridge in 1648.
ⓣ 257 320 112 ⓛ 10.00–22.00 Apr–Sept; 10.00–20.00 Mar & Oct;
10.00–18.00 Nov–Feb ⓝ Tram: 6, 9, 12, 22 to Újezd, then funicular.
Admission charge

Pražský hrad (Prague Castle)

According to the Guinness World Records, Prague Castle is the
largest ancient castle in the world. The huge hill-top complex on
Hradčanské náměstí includes dozens of architectural monuments
that provide some of the best views of town. The top sights in
the complex are St Vitus Cathedral, the Royal Palace, St George's
Basilica, The Picture Gallery, Mihulka Powder Tower and Golden Lane
(see individual listings that follow on pages 100–3). All except the
cathedral share the opening hours of the castle itself. It costs nothing
to walk around the complex, so you can explore the hulking exterior
of the castle and enjoy the beauty of all the buildings even if you're
tight on cash. It's a lovely place to wander around after dark as well,

◓ *Guards at Prague Castle*

as it's generally lit until midnight. If you do want to go into the museums and buildings, buy tickets at the Prague Castle Information Centre in the second courtyard after you pass through the main gate from Hradčanské náměstí. Tickets for the main attractions (excluding the St Vitus Cathedral, which is free to enter) are your best bargain at 350 Kč (500 Kč for families). ③ Hradčanské nám. ① 224 372 423 ◐ Castle: 05.00–00.00 summer; 06.00–23.00 winter; gardens: 10.00–20.00 Aug; 10.00–19.00 June & July; 10.00–19.00 May & Sept; 10.00–18.00 Apr & Oct; ticketed attractions: 09.00–18.00 summer; 09.00–16.00 winter ◎ Metro: Malostranská, then tram: 22 to Pražský hrad or Pohořelec

Chrám sv. Víta (St Vitus Cathedral)

Chrám sv. Víta was built in the year 926 as the court church of the Přemyslid princes and has since been the site for the coronation of Prague's kings and queens as well as the final resting place for royalty. The key parts of its Gothic construction were built in the 14th century, and the 18th and 19th centuries produced subsequent baroque and neo-Gothic additions. As you enter the cathedral through the back entrance into the main aisle, you'll notice the two central stained-glass windows, which depict the Holy Trinity, with the Virgin Mary to the left and Sv. Václav (St Wenceslas) kneeling to the right. The most interesting window in the cathedral was designed by the famous Czech art nouveau artist, Alfons Mucha. Of the massive Gothic cathedral's 21 chapels, the Svatováclavská kaple (St Wenceslas Chapel) is the most impressive. Encrusted with hundreds of pieces of jasper and amethyst and decorated with paintings from the 14th to the 16th centuries, this chapel houses the crown jewels and the tomb of Bohemia's patron saint, St Wenceslas. Just beyond this, the Kaple sv. Kříže (Chapel of the Holy Rood) leads to the entrance of the underground royal crypt where newly restored sarcophagi hold the remains of kings and their relatives. The centre sarcophagus is the final resting place of Karel IV (Charles IV), the Bohemian king who ruled during Prague's 'Golden Age'. In the back row are Charles's four wives (all placed in one sarcophagus), and in front of them is Jiří z Poděbrad (George of Poděbrady), the last king of Bohemia, who died in 1471.

Ⓦ www.hrad.cz ⏱ 09.00–18.00 Mon–Sat, 12.00–18.00 Sun, Mar–Oct; 09.00–16.00 Mon–Sat, 12.00–16.00 Sun, Nov–Feb

⬤ A detail of beautiful Mucha stained glass windows in St Vitus Cathedral

⬤ *Houses inside Prague Castle: no. 22 is where Kafka lived*

Kostel sv. Jiří (St George's Basilica)

Adjacent to the Royal Palace is Prague's oldest Romanesque structure, dating from the tenth century. It also houses Bohemia's first convent. No longer serving a religious function, the convent now contains relics of the castle's history and a gallery of Gothic Czech art.

Královský palác (Royal Palace)

The Royal Palace is where Bohemian kings and princes resided from the ninth century, and the vaulted Vladislavský sál (Vladislav Hall), once used for the coronation of kings, is now used for special occasions of state such as inaugurations of presidents and state visits.

Obrazárna Pražského hradu (Prague Castle Picture Gallery)

This gallery inside Prague Castle displays European and Bohemian masterpieces. The most celebrated is Hans von Aachen's *Portrait of a Girl* (1605–10), depicting the artist's daughter.

Prašná věž (Mihulka Powder Tower)

This building forms part of the northern bastion of the castle complex just off Golden Lane. Built as a defence tower in the late 15th century, it became a forger's workshop, where cannons and bells were made. It was turned into a laboratory for the 17th-century alchemists serving Emperor Rudolf II, and later became a gunpowder store. It is now a museum of alchemy, forging and Renaissance castle life.

Zlatá ulička (Golden Lane)

Within the castle complex is a chocolate-box row of tiny 16th-century houses built into the castle fortifications. Once home to castle sharp-shooters and artisans, the houses now contain small shops, galleries, snack bars, and boundless photo opportunities. Franz Kafka lived briefly at number 22. ❶ The lane is undergoing renovation works until May 2011

CULTURE

Kafka Museum

The life and work of Franz Kafka is displayed in photographs, manuscripts, diaries, correspondence and first editions, as well as audio-visual

programmes. 🅰 Cihelná 2b 📞 257 535 507 🆆 www.kafkamuseum.cz
🕙 10.00–18.00 Ⓜ Metro: Malostranská. Admission charge

MOZART & PRAGUE

In the late 18th century, Prague was a city to rival all others
in Europe. After surviving a devastating fire, the city burst
into a frenzy of renovation and redesign influenced by rich
German, Spanish and Italian noblemen. They left their
mark with incredible baroque-style palaces, churches
and gardens. The city's population grew to 100,000, and
as the economic situation improved, the stage was set for
artistic inspiration.

A Viennese Wunderkind named Wolfgang Amadeus
Mozart waltzed into Prague just as this artistic explosion
was at its height, and found here a skilled orchestra and an
appreciative audience. He moved into a beautiful villa named
Bertramka, to concentrate on his *magnum opus*. In the beautiful
gardens and baroque drawing rooms he found inspiration
and wrote one of his most famous operas. In 1787, the Estates
Theatre in Prague staged its premiere, and the world fell in
love with *Don Giovanni*.

As a result, on almost any day of the week you will find
some venue paying tribute to Mozart, one of Prague's most
famous adopted sons. It is worth attending at least one
performance; Czech musicians are some of the best in Europe,
the price is about half of what you'd pay in other European
venues, and even if you don't care for the music, you will not
fail to be inspired by the surroundings.

Museum Kampa

Once a mill, this museum displays beautiful collections of famous
Czech and Central European artists, such as Kupka and Gutfreund.
ⓐ U Sovových mlýnů 503/2 ⓣ 257 286 147 ⓦ www.museumkampa.cz
ⓛ 10.00–18.00 Ⓝ Metro: Malostranská. Admission charge

Šternberský palác (Šternberk Palace)

Adjacent to the main gate of Prague Castle, this gallery is also
known as the European Art Museum, as it displays an eclectic range
of just that spanning five centuries, from Orthodox iconography
to works by Rembrandt, El Greco, Goya and Van Dyck. If you have
time for only one museum during your stay, this is a good choice.
ⓐ Hradčanské nám. 15 ⓣ 233 090 570 ⓦ www.ngprague.cz
ⓛ 10.00–18.00 Tues–Sun Ⓝ Metro: Malostranská then tram: 22 to
Pražský hrad or Pohořelec. Admission charge

RETAIL THERAPY

Capriccio A noteworthy shop for sheet music. ⓐ Újezd 15
ⓣ 257 320 165 ⓛ 10.00–17.00 Mon–Sat Ⓝ Tram: Újezd

Elart Mostecká A sweet antiques gallery which sells genuine Czech
art from the 19th and 20th centuries as well as glassware, porcelain
and jewellery. ⓐ Mostecká 7 ⓣ 257 530 722 ⓦ www.antique-elart.cz
ⓛ 10.00–18.00 Ⓝ Metro: Malostranská

Material Glass shop with unique, upmarket pieces you can't
find anywhere else. ⓐ U Lužického semináře 7 ⓣ 257 530 046
ⓦ www.i-material.com ⓛ 10.30–21.00 Ⓝ Metro: Malostranská

Nový Smíchov A modern, sleek shopping centre that has everything for every taste. A great place for rainy-day window shopping. ⓐ Plzeňská 8 ⓣ 251 511 151 ⓛ 09.00–21.00 ⓝ Metro: Anděl

Shakespeare & Sons Thousands of hand-picked new and used English titles are to be found in this extensive bookshop. ⓐ U Lužického semináře 10 ⓣ 257 531 894 ⓦ www.shakes.cz ⓛ 11.00–19.00 ⓝ Metro: Malostranská

Truhlář Marionety An emporium for one-of-a-kind marionettes that deserve to become family treasures. ⓐ U Lužického semináře 10 ⓣ 257 531 894 ⓦ www.marionety.com ⓛ 11.00–19.00 ⓝ Metro: Malostranská

TAKING A BREAK

Café Savoy £ ❶ Fabulously French, with Edith Piaf resonating against the neo-Renaissance ceiling. Homemade pastries and cakes and foreign-language newspapers make this one of the nicest nooks in town. ⓐ Vítězná 5 ⓣ 257 311 562 ⓛ 08.00–22.30 Mon–Fri, 09.00–22.30 Sat & Sun ⓝ Tram: 22 to Újezd

Kafíčko £ ❷ Serves great coffee and teas in quiet, smoke-free surroundings just a street away from tourist mayhem. Let the world churn itself into a frenzy while you take the cake. ⓐ Míšeňská 10 ⓣ 724 151 795 ⓛ 10.00–22.00 ⓝ Metro: Malostranská

U Zavěšeného kafe £ ❸ 'At the Hanging Coffee' has long been associated with the Czech artists, musicians and intellectuals who frequent the place. 'Hanging a coffee' is local vernacular for

🔺 *Let Malá Strana dawn on you*

purchasing a coffee in advance for somebody who has yet to arrive. Hang out here for the coffee and for choice morsels like *satay* with peanut sauce, roast duck with cherry sauce, or traditional pickled *hermelín* (Czech Camembert). **ⓐ** Úvoz 6 **ⓣ** 257 532 868 **ⓦ** www.uzavesenyhokafe.cz **ⓛ** 11.00–00.00 **Ⓜ** Metro: Hradčanská, then tram: 22 to Pohořelec

● *Malá Strana serves it up with style*

Sovovy mlýny ££ ❹ Housed in the Museum Kampa (see page 105), this superb lunch spot by the Vltava enjoys panoramic views of Charles Bridge and the Old Town. ⓐ U Sovovych mlynů 503/2 ⓣ 724 699 565 ⓦ www.sovovymlyny.com ⓛ 11.00–23.00

AFTER DARK

RESTAURANTS
Česká hospoda £ ❺ The potato pancake pizzas are out of this world and there is great beer on tap. ⓐ Malostranské nám. 11 ⓣ 603 780 265 ⓦ www.ceskahospoda.cz ⓛ 10.00–23.30 ⓝ Metro: Malostranská

Haveli £ ❻ Authentic Indian cuisine in a beautiful cellar restaurant under vaulted ceilings with a good selection of vegetarian offerings. ⓐ Dejvická 6 ⓣ 233 344 800 ⓦ www.haveli.cz ⓛ 11.00–23.00 ⓝ Metro: Hradčanská

Malý Buddha £ ❼ Intimate and non-smoking Asian eatery in an easy-to-miss location as you're walking from the castle. Do yourself a favour: don't miss it. ⓐ Úvoz 46 ⓣ 220 513 894 ⓦ www.malybuddha.cz ⓛ 12.00–22.30 Tues–Sun ⓝ Metro: Hradčanská, then tram: 22 to Pohořelec

Bar Bar ££ ❽ A great ambience pervades this intimate, quirky restaurant, and the contemporary artworks are fun to browse while you wait for the chef to whip you up some traditional Czech duck or a filled pancake. ⓐ Vsehrdová 17 ⓣ 257 312 246 ⓦ www.bar-bar.cz ⓛ 12.00–00.00 Sun–Thur, 12.00–02.00 Fri & Sat ⓝ Tram: 22 to Újezd

Hergetova cihelna ££ ❾ This swish, contemporary eatery on
the banks of the Vltava has a cutting-edge feel, a low-light lounge
upstairs and a terrace boasting unrivalled views of Charles Bridge.
ⓐ Cihelná 2B ❶ 257 535 534 ⓦ www.kampagroup.com ● 11.30–01.00
ⓝ Metro: Malostranská

Olympia ££ ❿ Serves great Czech food up until midnight in the
atmosphere of a 1930s Czech watering hole. Pick from a menu of
traditional potato soup, smoked sausages and baked aromatic lamb,
all complemented perfectly by the excellent Pilsner lager on tap.
ⓐ Vítězná 7 ❶ 251 511 080 ⓦ www.kolkovna.cz ● 11.00–00.00
ⓝ Tram: 22 to Újezd

Restaurant La Bastille ££ ⓫ A laid-back French restaurant with
excellent food and atmosphere. Lamb, pork, fish, mussels and
frogs' legs are all served with flair. ⓐ Újezd 26/426 ❶ 257 312 830
ⓦ www.labastille.cz ● 12.00–01.00 ⓝ Tram: 22 to Újezd

U Sedmi švábů ££ ⓬ 'At the Seven Cockroaches' is a medieval
experience, complete with cellar dining, fire-eating, duelling and
even torture as entertainment. Traditional recipes use only authentic
15th- and 16th-century ingredients, so no tomatoes or potatoes.
ⓐ Jánský vršek 14 ❶ 257 531 455 ⓦ www.svabove.cz ● 11.00–23.00
ⓝ Metro: Malostranská, then tram: 22 to Malostranské nám.

Palffy Palace £££ ⓭ The ambience of this antique, turn-of-the-
century dining room is shabby chic, and a must for those wanting
to have a posh Central European dining experience. Views of the
castle gardens are free. ⓐ Valdštejnská 14 ❶ 257 530 522
ⓦ www.palffy.cz ● 11.00–23.00 ⓝ Metro: Malostranská

BARS & CLUBS

JJ Murphy's They have Guinness in this Irish bar, so grab a stool or get a couch-potato view of live sport in the attic lounge room. ⓐ Tržiště 4 ⓣ 257 535 575 ⓦ www.jjmurphys.cz ⓛ 09.00–01.00 ⓝ Metro: Malostranská, then tram: 22 to Malostranské nám.

Klub Lávka A firm Prague favourite, 'Club Avalanche' facilities include five themed dancing rooms, a café, restaurant and many themed bars on different levels. ⓐ Novotného Lávka 1 ⓣ 221 082 299 ⓦ www.lavka.cz ⓛ 21.30–05.00 ⓝ Metro: Malostranská

U Černého Vola 'At the Black Bull' is a short walk west of the castle. One of the best and cheapest pubs in the area, known for its excellent dark beer, but not for food. ⓐ Loretánské nam. 1 ⓣ 220 513 481 ⓛ 09.00–22.00 ⓝ Metro: Hradčanská, then tram: 22 to Brušnice

U Krále Brabantského A much-loved Prague pub, dating back to 1475! King Wenceslas IV, Mozart and the famous Renaissance alchemist, Edward Kelly, are said to have drunk here so why not follow in their footsteps? The tightly packed benches are liveliest in the evenings when the tankards come accompanied by some of Bohemia's best soak-up material. ⓐ Tuhovská 15 ⓣ 257 217 032 ⓦ www.brabant.cz ⓛ 12.00–00.00 ⓝ Metro: Malostranská, then tram: 22 to Malostranské nám.

U Malého Glena 'At Little Glen's' has been serving up strong coffee and cool jazz on Prague's Left Bank for a long time. Thankfully, they're still going strong, so you can see live bands almost every night, or at least sit and chat in this friendly jazz cellar/café. ⓐ Karmelitská 23 ⓣ 257 531 717 ⓦ www.malyglen.cz ⓛ 10.00–02.00 Mon–Fri, 10.00–02.30 Sat & Sun ⓝ Metro: Malostranská

Vinohrady, Vyšehrad & Žižkov

Once upon a time, this area was a vineyard. Voted the city's 'best neighbourhood to live in', Vinohrady is now a great combination of city-centre amenities, handsome art nouveau apartment buildings, and tourist-free tranquillity, based around Náměstí Míru square. Wenceslas Square (see page 62) is just a short stroll down Vinohradská, but the hustle and bustle of touristville seems a world away. Boasting some excellent neighbourhood cafés, pubs and restaurants, as well as some striking architecture, Vinohrady is sure to please. Vyšehrad is the final resting place of some of Prague's most famous artists and is also home to some amazing Czech Cubist architecture. Žižkov is Vinohrady's rowdy neighbour on the other side of the tracks. Once an open space where they buried Prague's plague victims, it is now anything but dead. Home to a large Romany population and historically one of the city's poorer districts, it is now up and coming; its counter-culture attracts expat hipsters and party animals from all over the globe.

All three districts developed in an optimistic era in the second half of the 19th century, when Czechoslovakia was trying to shrug off its identity crisis and take pride in its cultural heritage. Among the main attractions of this area are the quiet gardens, plentiful pubs, idiosyncratic clubs, and the strangest-looking TV tower you've ever seen. This proud presentation of neighbourhoods is where you will see how the real Prague lives, and, at night, how the real Prague parties.

SIGHTS & ATTRACTIONS

Havlíčkovy sady

Prague's second-largest park is located about seven blocks south of Náměsti Míru. Its most notable landmark is the beautiful Villa

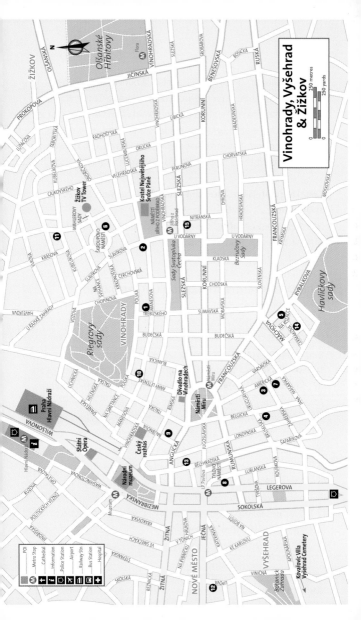

Gröbe (Grébovka), a neo-Renaissance villa built in 1871–88 as a luxury summer house for the industrialist, Moritz Gröbe. This is a perfect place to shake out the picnic blanket and drench yourself in the ambience of the graceful gardens that feature a working, if small, vineyard. Ⓝ Metro: Nám. Míru, then tram: 4 or 22 to Ruska and walk about three blocks west to the park entrance

Kostel Nejsvětějšího Srdce Páně (Church of the Most Sacred Heart of Our Lord)

This daring but beautiful piece of architecture was created by Slovene architect, Josip Plečnik, responsible for the functionalist

GRAND ARCHITECTURAL TOUR OF VINOHRADY

Real art nouveau enthusiasts should plan a walk that begins at the Vinohrady Theatre at Náměstí Míru (Peace Square) to see some of Prague's grandest residential streets. Walk down Římská and turn right on to Italská to see beautiful sculptures, wrought-iron balconies, coloured tiles and glass decorations. At Italská 20, have a look at the house marked 'V Černochově' ('In the Dark Continent'), which features huge lion heads. Continuing along Italská turn right onto Polská, which is quite possibly Prague's prettiest residential street. Chopinova, on the left, has some art nouveau buildings at numbers 4, 6, 8 and 14. Take a right along Na Švihance, and nearly every house is a work of art. One street over to the right, Krkonošská, has several houses with large sculptures and reliefs, the best one being old father Krakonoš leaning from the corner of Čerchovská. Ⓝ Metro: Nám. Míru or Jiřího z Poděbrad

🔺 *Kovařovic Villa – Cubist but not square*

renovation of Prague Castle in the 1920s. The most striking feature is the oversized transparent clock, meant to mimic a Gothic rose window, which looks as if it would fit a building twice the size. The exterior is a mix of imitated architectural styles but, as with the majority of functionalist churches, the interior is disappointingly plain. ⓐ Nám. Jiřího z Poděbrad ⓣ 222 727 713 ⓦ www.srdcepane.cz ⓛ 08.00–18.00; services: 09.00, 11.00, 18.00 Sun ⓝ Metro: Jiřího z Poděbrad

Kovařovic Villa

If you're interested in Czech Cubist architecture, this house is a must-see. Josef Chochol's (1880–1956) architectural creation echoes

⬥ *Prague's Žižkov TV Tower by night*

a Cubist painting. Houses nearby are equally whimsical. To the right is the Modernist Sequens Villa by Otakar Novotný (1912–13), and on the left is a neoclassical villa by Emil Kralicek (1912–13). Unfortunately, none of these homes are open to visitors, but they're definitely worth an exterior look. ⓐ Libušina 3 ⓝ Metro: Vyšehrad

Vyšehrad Cemetery

Some of Prague's most famous people rest at the Vyšehrad Cemetery. Open year-round, it's a perfect lookout and diversion from the madness of the city, offering you a calm, shady place in which to contemplate life. Access is through two gates at either end of the Church of St Peter and St Paul, where you will find a map of the tombs of the most well-known of those buried within. In the centre of the cemetery are individual plots among the beautifully appointed tombs and mausoleums, and at the end of a wide avenue is the Slavín, or Pantheon. Built in 1890, this massive tomb is dedicated to the most honoured figures in the Czech Republic, such as Antonín Dvořák, Alfons Mucha, Jan Neruda and Bedřich Smetana. The family tomb of ex-president Václav Havel is also here. ⓐ V Pevnosti 159 ⓘ 224 919 815 ⓛ 08.00–19.00 May–Sept; 08.00–18.00 Mar, Apr & Oct; 08.00–17.00 Nov–Feb ⓝ Metro: Vyšehrad

Žižkov TV Tower

Rising like a futuristic spaceship above the working-class quarter of Žižkov, this is one of Prague's most interesting, if controversial, buildings. At 216 m (708 ft), the TV tower is the tallest building in the city, and they say that on a clear day you can see it from a full 100 km (60 miles) away. Often regarded as a relic of the Communist era, the tower was actually completed after the Velvet Revolution in 1992. Although it's no longer possible to climb the tower, it's still a spectacular sight when seen from the ground or at a distance. Artist David Černý's black, computer-inspired babies climbing up the side of the tower lend a bit of whimsy to the structure. Also make sure you check out the beautifully haunting Jewish cemetery off to the side. Mahlerovy sady 1 Metro: Jiřiho z Poděbrad

CULTURE

Divadlo na Vinohradech (Vinohrady Theatre)
This is Vinohrady's grandest art nouveau building, constructed between 1904 and 1907. Statues depicting 'Truth' and 'Bravery' stand on top of the theatre's façade. Catch a ballet performance if you can; the drama is all Czech. Nám. Míru 7 224 257 601 www.dnv-praha.cz Box office: 11.00–19.00 Mon–Fri, 13.00–19.00 Sat Metro: Nám. Míru

RETAIL THERAPY

Aladin-Shop Not entirely typical of Prague but interesting nonetheless, this shop is crammed full of water pipes. Husitská 13 733 264 061 www.aladin-shop.cz 10.00–18.00 Mon–Fri Metro: Florenc

Boom Bap Shop Hip-hop record shop in a real, working-class neighbourhood. Bělehradská 57 777 904 950 11.00–20.00 Mon–Fri, 11.00–19.00 Sat, 12.00–18.00 Sun Metro: Nám. Míru

Cellarius Specialist wine shop offering more than 1,000 varieties from around the world; a perfect place to buy something nice to sip in one of the many parks to be found in Vinohrady. Budečská 29

⬤ *Palác Flora shopping centre*

① 222 515 243 ⓦ www.cellarius.cz ⓛ 10.30–23.00 Mon–Fri, 10.30–18.00 Sat ⓝ Metro: Nám. Míru

Palác Flora This encompasses about 120 reasonably priced shops on four floors, plus a supermarket and an IMAX cinema. ⓐ Vinohradská 151 ① 255 741 712 ⓦ www.palacflora.cz ⓛ 09.00–21.00 Mon–Sat, 10.00–21.00 Sun ⓝ Metro: Flora

Parthenonas Sells Greek wines, olives and other yummy products. ⓐ Vinohradská 66 ① 724 296 357 ⓛ 10.00–19.00 Mon–Thur, 10.00–18.00 Fri ⓝ Metro: Jiřího z Poděbrad

Rybanaruby Go with the flow at the 'Inside-out Fish', a multimedia saloon that combines a performance stage, shop and tea house with free internet access. Good used CDs and unique arts and crafts are for sale. Manesova 87 731 570 701 www.rybanaruby.net 10.00–22.00 Mon–Sat Metro: Jiřího z Poděbrad

Shakespeare & Sons Just outside the city centre, S&S offers some excellent reads in a real residential neighbourhood. Kitted out with a comfortable coffee bar up front where you can sit all day, this is the perfect place to review the newest literary finds. At weekends, live bands often play. Krymska 12 271 740 839 www.shakes.cz 12.00–19.00 Metro: Nám. Míru, then tram: 22 to Krymská

TAKING A BREAK

Ambiente £ ❶ Located well off the tourist track, Prague's most successful wholly Czech-owned restaurant. Forego pastas in favour of real Argentine Angus, or tender beef ribs and spicy chicken wings, served up with tangy sauces. Mánesova 59 222 727 851 www.ambi.cz 11.00–00.00 Mon–Fri, 12.00–00.00 Sat & Sun Metro: Nám. Míru

Bio Potraviny – Zdravá Výživa £ ❷ Small health-food store on the square. In addition to tofu and soy products, they also sell fresh bread and cookies. Nám. Jiřího z Poděbrad 4 222 723 602 09.00–17.00 Mon–Fri Metro: Jiřího z Poděbrad

Blatouch £ ❸ Tasty salads, sandwiches, pasta dishes and a range of desserts together with free Wi-Fi at the 'Buttercup' café and bookshop. Americká 17 222 328 643 www.blatouch.cz 10.00–00.00

Mon–Thur, 10.00–01.00 Fri, 11.00–01.00 Sat, 11.00–00.00 Sun
Ⓝ Metro: Nám. Míru

Medúza £ ❹ Cosy café with a friendly retro atmosphere, comfortable
old chairs, and decent coffee, teas and light meals. The savoury
palačinky (pancakes) are a favourite. ⓐ Belgická 17 ❶ 222 515 107
Ⓦ www.meduza.cz ❸ 10.00–01.00 Mon–Fri, 12.00–01.00 Sat & Sun
Ⓝ Metro: Nám. Míru

U Dědka £ ❺ Chilled-out atmosphere for latte-sipping in the café
upstairs or digging into some world foods downstairs. A menu
to please all tastes, with cheap lunch specials. ⓐ Na Kozacce 12
❶ 222 522 784 ❸ 11.00–01.00 Mon–Fri, 16.00–01.00 Sat & Sun
Ⓝ Metro: Nám. Míru, then tram: 4, 22 to Krymská

U Sadu £ ❻ A block from the TV Tower, with everyday Czech dishes
and antiques displayed at all angles. Its late opening hours make
this a great stopover during an evening out. ⓐ Škroupovo nám. 5
❸ 08.00–02.00 Mon–Wed & Sun, 08.00–04.00 Thur–Sat
Ⓝ Metro: Jiřího z Poděbrad

Zanzibar £ ❼ Filling breakfasts and light savoury fare served all day
in a tastefully decorated space off a quiet square. Friendly service and a
good wine list. ⓐ Americká 15 ❶ 222 520 315 Ⓦ www.kavarnazanzibar.cz
❸ 08.00–23.00 Mon–Fri, 10.00–23.00 Sat & Sun Ⓝ Metro: Nám. Míru

Irish Pub Martin's £–££ ❽ Don't groan – this place is popular
with locals as well as tourists and serves great steaks as well as a
good range of vegetarian options. ⓐ Lublaňská 57/5 ❶ 222 518 140
❸ 11.00–23.30 Mon–Fri, 12.00–23.30 Sat & Sun Ⓝ Metro: I. P. Pavlova

Balbínova poetická hospůdka ££ ❾ Come for great food, a relaxed
ambience and a busy programme of cultural events. ❸ Balbínova 6
❶ 723 889 143 Ⓦ www.balbinka.cz ⓛ 17.00–00.00 Mon–Fri,
18.00–00.00 Sat & Sun Ⓝ Metro: Muzeum

AFTER DARK

RESTAURANTS

Amigos £ ❿ Prague's most authentic Mexican eatery, with walls
bedecked in sombreros and B&W photos of *bandidos* and colourful
Aztec-style blankets without appearing kitsch. Feast on large portions of
enchiladas, *burritos*, *quesadillas* and *tacos* washed down with good
old Czech ale. ❸ Anny Letenské 16 ❶ 222 250 594 Ⓦ www.amigos.cz
ⓛ 11.30–00.00 Ⓝ Metro: Muzeum then tram: 11 to Italská

Palác Akropolis £ ⓫ One of Prague's best venues, right under
the Žižkov TV Tower, with a concert hall, restaurant, café and two
bars under one roof. You'll come for the great food and drinks,
and leave much later than you think. Ask the doorman to call you
a taxi. ❸ Kubelíkova 27 ❶ 296 330 912 Ⓦ www.palacakropolis.cz
ⓛ Café: 10.00–00.00 Mon–Fri, 16.00–00.00 Sat & Sun; restaurant:
11.00–00.30; bar: 21.00–05.00 Ⓝ Metro: Jiřího z Poděbrad

Pivovarský Dům £ ⓬ A pub with its own microbrewery on site. Along
with typical Czech-style beer, the company also brews fruit beers
similar to those popular in Belgium. Good Czech restaurant serving
all the classics, including *Pivní sýr*, a strong, pungent cheese that you
mix with onions and a drop of beer to make a spread to eat on toasted
bread. ❸ Lipová 15 ❶ 296 216 666 Ⓦ www.gastroinfo.cz/pivodum
ⓛ 11.00–23.30 Ⓝ Metro: I. P. Pavlova or Karlovo nám.

Café Radost FX ££ ⑬ Prague's premier hotspot combines vegetarian dining in the restaurant, an underground house club, and a comfortable Asian-inspired lounge to take in the sights and sounds. A firm favourite with expats, locals and those in the know. Their wicked Sunday brunch is the best hangover cure on earth. ⓐ Bělehradská 120 ⓣ 603 193 711 ⓦ www.radostfx.cz ⓛ 10.00–03.00 ⓝ Metro: I. P. Pavlova

Louis Armstrong ££ ⑭ This cosily kitsch but popular theme restaurant in the heart of Vinohrady serves quality international and Czech dishes to relaxing jazz tones. ⓐ Čermákova 4 ⓣ 224 251 671 ⓛ 11.00–23.00 ⓝ Metro: Nám. Míru, then tram: 4 or 22 to Jana Masaryka

Mozaika ££ ⑮ It may be outside the city centre, but it's worth the trip. International fusion with flair and an airy interior. ⓐ Nitranská 13 ⓣ 224 253 011 ⓦ www.restaurantmozaika.cz ⓛ 11.30–00.00 Mon–Fri, 12.00–00.00 Sat, 16.00–00.00 Sun ⓝ Metro: Jiřího z Poděbrad, then tram: 10 or 16 to Vinohradská vodárna

CLUBS & BARS

Le Clan As gloriously seedy as it gets, this spectacular DJ dive hits its stride in the wee hours with the drag queens. If you can get past the dodgy characters at the door, head downstairs to meet other lounge lizards or move further downstairs to play a quick game of ping pong. Mirrors in the toilets hang suspiciously horizontal. ⓐ Balbínova 23 ⓣ 222 251 226 ⓦ www.leclan.cz ⓛ 02.00–mid-morning Wed–Sun (i.e. Tues–Sat nights) ⓝ Metro: Muzeum

Gejzee..r The largest gay club in Prague is cavernous and sweaty, with big dance floors and twin bars serving to all sorts, including

straights. Vinohradská 40 ☏ 222 516 036 🕔 21.00–05.00 Thur–Sat
Ⓝ Metro: Nám. Míru

Hapu Friendly, unpretentious cocktails in cosy comfort. Get here early
enough to find couch space. Ⓐ Orlická 8 ☏ 222 720 158 🕔 18.00–02.00
Mon–Sat Ⓝ Metro: Flora, or Tram: 11 to Radhošťská

Music Club 77 The origin of the name '77' is a mystery, but if you
want a good old cheesy disco, this is definitely the place to come.
Ⓐ Velehradská 26 ☏ 605 440 260 Ⓦ www.musicclub77.com
🕔 18.00–late Mon–Sat Ⓝ Metro: Jiřího z Poděbrad

Termix One of the most popular clubs on the gay/lesbian scene. The
lounge has a contemporary interior, modern glass bar, small dance
floor, comfortable sofas and dark rooms. Inhibition-free. Open late.
Ⓐ Třebízského 4 ☏ 222 710 462 Ⓦ www.club-termix.cz 🕔 20.00–05.00
Wed–Sun Ⓝ Metro: Jiřího z Poděbrad

U Vystřelenýho oka The beers never cease at this thoroughly local pub
that serves hearty and cheap grub to a mixed crowd of backpackers
and yuppies. Ⓐ U božích bojovníků 3 ☏ 222 540 465 Ⓦ www.uvoka.cz
🕔 16.30–01.00 or later Ⓝ Metro: Florenc, then tram: 5, 9 or 26
to Husinecká

Valentino Popular with the gay and lesbian crowd, this relaxed
nightspot is generally free of charge. Ⓐ Vinohradská 40 ☏ 222 513 491
Ⓦ www.club-valentino.cz 🕔 21.00–late Sun–Thur, 22.00–late Fri & Sat
Ⓝ Metro: Nam. Míru

▶ *Autumn colours in Karlštejn*

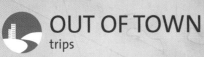

OUT OF TOWN
trips

Karlštejn

Situated 29 km (18 miles) southwest of Prague, Karlštejn makes a perfect day trip from the city, as it's close enough to Prague for you to spend the day castle-gazing in the fresh air and still make it back in time to enjoy the city nightlife. The magic of Karlštejn is that it's something typically Czech: a fairytale castle bang in the middle of some truly gorgeous countryside. It's popular with tourists and Czechs alike, as evidenced by the visitor records – more than a quarter of a million people visit it each year – so try to arrive there early to beat the crowds.

Charles IV built the castle between 1348 and 1357 as a place of rest and relaxation, and as a fortress to safeguard the crown jewels of the Holy Roman Empire. In the period of Charles's reign, it took one day by horse to reach Prague, where the European political élite would meet. Through the hard work of renovation teams, what we see now is a perfectly preserved medieval castle, without any Gothic ornamentation.

The castle is a good place to visit if you can get in on a tour, but just walking around its exterior is more than enough to capture the ambience of the place. As you walk up the hill towards the castle, you are immediately rewarded by the view spread out in front of you: picture-perfect rolling hills, the town and river. The townspeople have got used to seeing gaping visitors distractedly walking around, and many have set up shop right in their front yards, where you can browse and buy at your leisure.

GETTING THERE

By rail
The best (and only) way to get to Karlštejn with public transport is by taking the train from Smíchov Station (◐ Metro: Smíchovské

nádraží). It leaves regularly throughout the day and takes about 45 minutes to reach Karlštejn.

By road

The quickest route by car takes about half an hour. Follow the E50 out of Prague, heading towards Plzeň. Take the Beroun exit, and follow the signs along the Berounka River towards Karlštejn.

SIGHTS & ATTRACTIONS

Karlštejn Castle tours

Unless you have a particular interest in the subject, don't bother with the wax museum, Clock House, nativity museum or small fortress museum in Karlštejn village. These are tourist traps and, for most visitors, are not worth your while. Instead, go for a guided tour of Karlštejn Castle which will take you through some interesting rooms and buildings. Tour One includes the Imperial Palace, Hall of Knights, Chapel of St Nicholas, Royal Bedroom and the Audience Hall. Tour Two includes all of Tour One plus the Holy Rood Chapel, the Chapel of St Katherine and Church of Our Lady, and the library.

The prismatic Great Tower with the Holy Rood Chapel is the most valuable part of the complex. Decorated by semi-precious stones, set in the shapes of crosses, the chapel holds a unique collection of idealised portraits of saints, popes, bishops and spiritual teachers. Above the altar there is a niche encased with golden bars, which once held the crown jewels and relics. Looking up, you see a starry sky with the moon, the sun and the five planets, the only ones known at that time.

● *The Holy Rood Chapel at Karlštejn*

● *Head up to the castle tower for spectacular views*

You should book several months in advance by telephone or online if you wish to take Tour Two, noting that it is only offered June to October. Otherwise, you can buy tickets for the castle at the ticket information booth. Tour One costs 250 Kč for an adult, Tour Two is 300 Kč. The booth will also supply you with information about the town and events in the area. ❶ 311 681 617 ⓦ www.hradkarlstejn.cz ❶ 09.00–12.00 & 12.30–17.00 Tues–Sun, May, June & Sept; 09.00–12.00 & 12.30–18.00 July & Aug;

KARLŠTEJN GOLF CLUB

Established in 1993, Praha Karlštejn Golf Club hosted its first European PGA tour event in 1997. It serves up a challenging 18-hole, par-72 course on the hill just across the river from the castle and has some truly magnificent views. It is one of the few courses in the Czech Republic that really challenges a golfer's ability. It's an uphill course, so be prepared to lug your clubs up the slopes between holes. A game here is a bit expensive by Czech standards (green fees start at 2,000 Kč), but for golf enthusiasts it's worth it. There's also an excellent relaxation centre with restaurant, swimming pool, hot steam room and massages so you can treat yourself after a hard day on the greens. Reservations are required for weekends.
🕿 311 604 999 🔳 www.karlstejn-golf.cz 🕒 08.00–sunset

09.00–12.00 & 13.00–16.00 Apr & Oct; 09.00–12.00 & 13.00–15.00 Nov, Dec & Mar

TAKING A BREAK

Hotel Restaurace Koruna £ Sit inside or out on the main street; the terrace tables are usually full of people feasting on the large portions of Czech fare and on the great views. Friendly staff. 🅐 Karlštejn 13 🕿 311 681 465 🔳 www.korunakarlstejn.cz 🕒 09.30–22.00

Restaurace U Janů £ A shady terrace and reasonable prices make this basic Czech restaurant a favourite. Live music at weekends. 🅐 Karlštejn 28 🕿 311 681 210 🕒 09.30–22.00

U Elišky £ This Communist-era eatery is popular with tour buses, fills up at mealtimes in summer and serves large portions of stodgy Czech fare. ⓐ Karlštejn 99 ❶ 311 681 444 Ⓦ www.eliskakarlstejn.cz
Ⓛ 10.00–23.00

Restaurace Blanky z Valois ££ On the main street heading up to the castle, this place serves pizzas and has an extensive wine list, though you should sample some of the quaffable Karlštejn vintage.
ⓐ Karlštejn 140 ❶ 608 021 075 Ⓛ 11.00–22.00

ACCOMMODATION

Hotel Elma £ Situated 3 km (nearly 2 miles) from Karlštejn Castle, this hotel offers reasonable prices and reasonable digs. Great views of the pretty Berounka river valley. There is also a decent restaurant.
ⓐ Srbsko 179 ❶ 311 623 316 Ⓛ Restaurant: 10.00–22.00 Mon–Thur, 10.00–23.00 Fri & Sat, 10.00–21.00 Sun

Pension Pod dračí skálou £ Small and quaint with only three rooms, it's right under the dragon's cliff. ⓐ Karlštejn 130 ❶ 311 681 177

Hotel Karlštejn ££ Right in the centre of Karlštejn, this comfortable 4-star hotel has a restaurant with garden tables in the summer.
ⓐ Pod Hradem 7 ❶ 604 204 700 Ⓦ www.hotel-karlstejn.cz

Hotel Koruna ££ This 3-star hotel is in the centre of Karlštejn and the management speaks English. The large summer terrace has lovely views of the castle. ⓐ Karlštejn 13 ❶ 311 681 465
Ⓦ www.korunakarlstejn.cz

Romantický hotel Mlýn Karlštejn £££ A 4-star treat in an old mill –
the perfect place for a romantic overnight trip. The hotel is right on
the riverbank and makes a good base for bike and canoe trips on the
river. ⓐ Karlštejn 329 ⓣ 311 744 411 ⓦ www.hotelmlynkarlstejn.cz

🔺 *Karlštejn – it's all uphill from here*

Terezín (Theresienstadt)

Be warned: Terezín is a highly recommended and straightforward day trip from Prague, lying 48 km (30 miles) northwest of the city, but you will not want to linger for a nice lunch or stay overnight. In fact, after seeing what you'll see here, you'll want to ponder, and then leave. Even were it not for their barbaric use by the Nazis, the massive strongholds at Terezín (Theresienstadt in German) would still be a chilling sight.

Joseph II, son of Maria Theresa, built Terezín in 1866 as a fortress against Prussian attacks. The fortress was never used against the Prussians, so fell into disrepair and was used alternately as a garrison and jail and a World War I prisoner of war camp. Then the occupying Nazi forces moved in.

Terezín, dubbed 'Paradise Ghetto' by the Nazis, was not a place of execution or medical testing. Instead, it was a transit camp through which more than 140,000 people passed; more than half ended up at the death camps of Auschwitz and Treblinka. A town originally built to garrison 5,000, Terezín held 60,000 inmates at the height of the war. Of these, 35,000 died from starvation, disease or suicide before they could be carted off in trains to the other concentration camps. Russian forces liberated Terezín on 10 May 1945.

Today, the camp stands as a memorial to the dead and a monument to the dark side of humanity. But it is also an educational centre with a mission to inform people about this sad chapter in Czech history. Terezín Memorial staff became acutely aware of the absence of information regarding the Holocaust in Czech schools. In previous decades, under Communism, the topic was taboo and experts were few. Now the educational centre offers well-researched study materials to young people and adults to reopen this chapter of history, focusing on themes of interpersonal relationships, tolerance and human dignity in the context of racial equality.

GETTING THERE

By road

Terezín is a 45-minute drive north out of Prague towards Dresden on the main highway E55 (D8). Look for the Terezín exit signs. Buses leave hourly from either Florenc bus station or from outside Holešovice railway station. The ride takes about an hour, and a round-trip costs 130 Kč. See www.vlak-bus.cz for details.

▲ *An aerial photo of the camp at Terezín*

SIGHTS & ATTRACTIONS

Památník Terezín (Terezín Camp)

The camp is what you come to Terezín to see. Inside the Major Fortress the plain, empty streets are eerie. Just off the main square lies the Museum of the Ghetto, chronicling the rise of Nazism and life in the camp. The museum provides English pamphlets to describe the exhibits.

A ten-minute walk from the Major Fortress over the Ohře River takes you to the Minor Fortress. In front of the fortress's main

◐ *A memorial to the victims of the Holocaust*

ORGANISED TOURS

It may well be worth your while considering taking an organised tour that will collect you from Prague and inform and educate you about what you'll see in Terezín. Here are two tried and tested operators:

Martin Tours A good, informative five-hour tour. Their bus leaves from Prague's Staroměstské náměstí and costs 1,100 Kč for an adult. ⓐ Stepánská 61 ① 224 212 473 ⓦ www.martintour.cz ⓛ Tours leave at 09.30 Tues, Wed, Fri–Sun

Wittmann Tours An experienced company offering a seven-hour bus tour to the Terezín concentration camp. The bus leaves from Prague at Pařížská 28, near the Jewish Cemetery. The tour is 1,250 Kč for adults and 1,100 Kč for students. ⓐ Novotného Lávka 5 ① 222 252 472 ⓦ www.wittmann-tours.com ⓛ Tours leave 10.00 daily May–Oct; 10.00 Tues, Thur, Sat & Sun mid-Mar–Apr, Nov & Dec; private tours available Jan–mid-Mar

entrance is the Národní hřbitov (National Cemetery), where the bodies exhumed from the mass graves were given proper burials. As you enter the main gate, the sign above it, *Arbeit Macht Frei* ('Work Sets You Free'), is a depressing reminder of the self-righteousness that accompanied the appalling treatment of the people imprisoned here. You can walk through the Magdeburg prison barracks, execution grounds and cells. A combined entrance ticket gives you access to all parts of the camp and costs 200 Kč. ⓐ Principova alej 304 ① 416 782 225 ⓦ www.pamatnik-terezin.cz ⓛ 09.00–18.00 summer; 09.00–17.00 winter. Admission charge

WARTIME PUBLIC RELATIONS

Terezín is a haunting reminder of the cruel public relations hoax that SS Chief Heinrich Himmler played on the rest of the world just as it was waking up to news of Nazi atrocities. In 1944, three foreign observers (two from the International Red Cross) came to Terezín to find out if the rumours of what was happening to the Jews were true. The Germans carefully choreographed every detail of the visit so that the observers saw a clean town with a Jewish administration, banks, shops, cafés, schools and a thriving cultural life. Plays, recitals, concerts and even a jazz band kept up the charade. To remedy the overcrowded conditions, the Nazis transported 7,500 of the camp's sick and elderly prisoners to Auschwitz. The observers left with the impression that all was well. The trick inspired the Nazis to make a film of the camp: *A Town Presented to the Jews from the Führer*.

TAKING A BREAK

There are few places to eat in Terezín, and you may not want to stay here much longer than you have to. However, in the main parking lot you'll find a small stand where you can buy snacks and drinks. Inside the Major Fortress, near the museum, is a decent and inexpensive restaurant with standard Czech fare (🕐 10.00–21.00 Sun–Fri).

● *Rush-hour on Prague's metro*

Kolej 2	Směr	Směr	Kolej 1
	Stanice	Stanice	
	Háje	Nádraží	
		Holešovice	

PRACTICAL
information

Directory

GETTING THERE
By air
Almost every international carrier or their affiliate serves Prague Airport (see page 48), which is 20 km (12 miles) from the city centre. There are direct flights from major European and North American cities. Low-cost air carriers like bmi baby, easyJet, Jet2, Thomson and Ryanair, and discount ticket agencies such as Fly Europe, offer good discounts, especially if you book more than a month in advance. Check ⓦ www.bmibaby.com, ⓦ www.easyjet.com, ⓦ www.jet2.com, ⓦ www.thomsonfly.com, ⓦ www.ryanair.com and ⓦ www.flyeurope.com for details.

Many people are aware that air travel emits CO_2, which contributes to climate change. You may be interested in the possibility of lessening the environmental impact of your flight through **Climate Care** (ⓦ www.climatecare.org), which offsets your CO_2 by funding environmental projects around the world.

By rail
Travelling to Prague by rail is a fairly quick, easy and attractive option, particularly if you enjoy train travel. There are various routes from the UK or the rest of Europe, including taking the Cologne-Prague sleeper train or going via Paris and Berlin. See ⓦ www.seat61.com for reliable advice on the different options. The monthly *Thomas Cook European Rail Timetable* (ⓘ +44 1733 416 477 ⓦ www.thomascookpublishing.com) has up-to-date schedules for European international and national train services.

By road

To get to Prague from the UK by car, you will need to drive about 13 hours over 1,250 km (775 miles), as well as take a ferry or the Eurotunnel over to France. Coach journeys take longer, around 20 hours, but are much cheaper and easier. **Eurolines/National Express** (+44 8717 818181 www.eurolines.co.uk) offer regular coach services to Prague from London for about £65 each way. **Student Agency** (841 101 101 wwww.studentagency.cz) operates a similar coach service, with prices hovering around £70 for a single ticket and £105 for a return.

ENTRY FORMALITIES

As a member of the EU and the Schengen zone, the Czech Republic allows nationals of Australia, Canada, Japan, New Zealand, the USA and many other countries to visit the Czech Republic for up to 90 days without a visa. Citizens of EU countries including the UK can officially stay for 30 days without registering their stay with the police. South Africans are among those who must obtain a Schengen visa in their home country before arrival. To see what your current visa status is, visit www.mvcr.cz.

MONEY

The Czech Republic is a member of the EU, but the currency is still the Czech crown (CZK), written Kč or *koruna*. Optimists claim the euro will replace the crown by 2015, although some speculate it will be as late as 2019. Banknotes come in denominations of 50, 100, 200, 500, 1,000, 2,000 and 5,000 crowns. There are numerous ATM machines which accept Visa, MasterCard, Maestro, Visa Debit and American Express cards. If you have to exchange money, you can find the best rates at Xchange offices near the Old Town Square, or at any bank.

If you are a visitor from a non-EU country, you can reclaim up to 17 per cent of the value-added tax (DPH), provided you spend at least 2,000 Kč in a single shop and stay in the Czech Republic for fewer than 30 days. See Ⓦ www.globalrefund.com for information.

HEALTH, SAFETY & CRIME

The good news: the water is safe to drink and smoking is prohibited at schools, cinemas, theatres, sports facilities, state offices and other public spaces such as bus and tram stops. (Do not smoke while waiting for your tram; you will incur an on-the-spot 1,000 Kč fine.) The bad news: the air isn't very healthy to breathe on some days, especially in the autumn and winter, when smog settles over the city. If you suffer from asthma, make sure you bring your inhaler with you.

Prague is very safe to walk at all times of the day or night, and almost everyone uses public transport. Assaults are very rare, perhaps due to the visible police presence that tends to snuff out any problems before they arise. But Prague is a city, and therefore any tourist is a target. Pickpockets are very skilful, working in groups to distract and then rob unwary travellers as they ride the tram or metro. If a tram or metro compartment looks packed, don't squish in: just wait for the next train. If you go to a busy restaurant or stay at a touristy hotel, watch for double-charging.

Swindles abound in Prague, but you'll be happy to know there's a way to fight back. If you've encountered waiters who voluntarily determine the tip by adding it to the bill, taxi drivers who overcharge or hotels that treat you badly, call the **Czech Retail Inspection Office** (ⓐ Štěpánská 15 ⓣ 296 366 219 Ⓦ www.coi.cz ⓛ 09.00–17.00

🔺 *Petřín Hill in the springtime*

🔺 *Trams are a good way to explore the city*

Mon–Fri). They may not be able to help in your individual case but they can send out inspectors and can prevent it happening to others. Be sure to keep the receipt or note the details of the company involved when lodging a complaint.

OPENING HOURS

Clothing shops and grocery stores in Prague are generally open Monday through Saturday from 10.00 to 18.00. Some close by 14.00 at weekends, and many don't open on Sunday at all.

Restaurants are open generally every day from 11.00 to 22.00, but don't be surprised if they close earlier in winter. Pubs usually open every day at 17.00 and stay open at least until 23.00. Clubs stay open much longer, often until the early hours of the morning.

TOILETS

There aren't many free public toilets in Prague and even the usually civilised McDonald's charges to use the facilities. Unless you splash out for an admission ticket to a cultural landmark or eat at a restaurant, you will have to cough up 5 Kč to use a bathroom, rough paper included. Paying toilets, labelled 'WC', are located at underground metro stations and along the tourist route.

CHILDREN

Prague is a very child-friendly city, with many parks to play in and child-oriented things to do and see. Prague's babies are well catered for, and you can find a wide variety of nappies and all sorts of baby accoutrements in any local baby shop or *drogerie* (pharmacy). Generally, however, Czechs believe that children should be seen and not heard, and are not used to seeing them in fancy restaurants, expensive shops or at the opera. If you do decide to bring your small child to a cultural event, make sure that you are well armed with quiet anti-boredom ammunition to entertain them while you have fun. Another plus for children under six – entrance to most museums is free. If you are staying in Prague with your children and are not sure how to keep them entertained, here are a few activities that may do the trick.

Prague Zoo (📧 U Trojského zámku 3/120 📞 296 112 111 🌐 www.zoopraha.cz 🕐 09.00–17.00, Mar; 09.00–18.00 Apr, May, Sept & Oct; 09.00–19.00 June–Aug; 09.00–16.00 Nov–Feb 🚇 Metro: Nádraži Holešovice, then bus: 112 or free shuttle bus weekends & public holidays Apr–Sept. Admission charge), located near the Trója Chateau on the outskirts of Prague, is a fun option, particularly if you take the 75-minute boat ride to get there. Boats depart from Rašínovo nábř. embankment (between the Palackého and Jiraskův bridges) at 09.30, 12.30 and 15.30 from March to October. Tickets are 140 Kč for an adult and 70 Kč for a child. The boat also runs from the zoo back to the centre, departing at 11.00, 14.00 and 17.00. See 🌐 www.paroplavba.cz for details.

Another fun excursion can be had on **Nostalgická Tramvaj 91** (Nostalgic Tram No. 91 📞 296 124 902). This historic tram runs at weekends and holidays through all the most beautiful Prague locales from April to mid-November. It leaves hourly from 12.00 to 18.00 and is a cheap (35 Kč) and cheerful way to cover a lot of ground without wearing out little legs.

Younger children will adore the famous **Divadlo Spejbla a Hurvínka** theatre (📧 Dejvická 38 📞 224 316 784 🌐 www.spejbl-hurvinek.cz 🚇 Metro: Hradčanská. Admission charge). Its clowns and stupid stunts will keep you laughing. The best of the black light theatre experiences can be found in the **Image Theatre** (📧 Pařižska 4 📞 222 314 448 🌐 www.imagetheatre.cz 🕐 Box office: 09.00–20.00 Mon–Sat, 10.00–Sun 🚇 Metro: Staroměstská. Admission charge) while the **Muzeum Hraček** (Toy Museum 📧 Jirska ul. 6 📞 224 372 294 🕐 09.30–17.30 Apr–Nov 🚇 Metro: Hradčanská) at Prague Castle is the second-largest exhibition of toys in the world.

There are parks for children in the Malá Strana side of town.

⬥ *The kids will enjoy taking a pedalo on the Vltava*

Kampa Park and Kampa Island right under Charles Bridge provide shady nap-time retreats, pedal boat rentals, and playgrounds.

COMMUNICATIONS
Internet
High-speed internet cafés dot the city, and these are just two of the best:

Blue Mail Internet café and gallery in the Old Town. ⓐ Konviktska 8 ⓒ 10.00–22.00 Mon–Fri, 10.00–23.00 Sat & Sun ⓜ Metro: Staroměstská

Pl@neta Very cheap rates for surfing the net. ⓐ Vinohradská 102 ⓘ 267 311 182 ⓒ 08.00–23.00 ⓜ Metro: Jiřího z Poděbrad

Phone
Public telephones are either coin- or card-operated. You can buy

TELEPHONING THE CZECH REPUBLIC

To phone Prague from abroad, enter your country's dialling code, followed by the international country code (420) and the local nine-digit number. Some of the most used dialling codes are: Australia (0011); Canada (011); New Zealand (00); South Africa (00); UK (00); USA (011).

TELEPHONING ABROAD

To call abroad from the Czech Republic, dial 00, then the country code, regional code (usually omitting the first 0) and finally the local number you require. Some of the most used country codes are: Australia (61); Canada (1); New Zealand (64); South Africa (27); UK (44); USA (1).

The number for the international operator is ☎ 1181.

telephone cards in post offices, newsagents and kiosks or tobacco stores. For international calls, you can buy a pre-paid card at the above-mentioned places; this option costs significantly less than using coins to make calls.

Almost everyone in Prague has a mobile phone. If you decide to bring your mobile phone from home, make sure you enable your roaming programme so that you can receive calls once you're in Prague. If you plan to make a lot of calls, it may be cheaper to purchase a local SIM card for your phone.

Post

If you want to send packages back home, use the **Main Post Office** on Jindrišská 14 (🕐 10.00–13.00, 13.30–16.00 Mon–Fri) across the street from the Obecní dům (Municipal House). You can buy stamps at the post office, or any *tabák* (tobacconist) or information centre in town. Česká pošta (Czech Postal Service) post boxes are orange with two mail slots; you can put the mail in on either side.

An airmail letter takes about a week to reach its overseas destination; a surface mail package could take up to three months to arrive.

ELECTRICITY

The electrical current in the Czech Republic is 220 V with standard, continental round two-pin plugs and earthed, three-pin plugs. A two-pin plug will fit in a three-pin socket. Visitors from the UK, America and Canada will require plug adaptors, obtainable at the airport or from any electrical or department store. If you forget to bring one, ask at your hotel.

TRAVELLERS WITH DISABILITIES

Visitors (and residents) with disabilities don't have it very easy in Prague, with its high kerbs and cobbled streets – but things are changing fast. A very useful source of information is the portal Ⓦ www.praha.eu – click on 'Life in Prague' then 'Disabled Persons' for up-to-date news, contacts and information aimed at visitors with disabilities. The PIS website (see page 151) allows you to search for 'barrier free' venues in Prague – click on 'Addresses' to access the search engine.

Trains marked 'S' are accessible for wheelchair users but it's best to call **Czech Railways** (ⓘ (420) 840 112 113 Ⓦ www.cd.cz) at least a day in advance to arrange your trip. Some metro stations have disabled access and these are all well marked on most public transport/metro maps. Larger hotels and restaurants and

Vstup výtah

Metro C Wilsonova ul.

Metro A Vinohradská ul.

Muzeum

C

A

🔺 *Some metro stations have disabled access*

attractions in tourist areas are becoming increasingly accessible.
If you are worried about access, it's best to call an English-speaking
manager and make sure your needs are fully understood
before arriving.

TOURIST INFORMATION

The official Czech tourist board is Czech Tourism. There are two offices:

🄰 Vinohradska 46 ❶ 221 580 516 ⓦ www.czechtourism.cz
🕓 08.30–12.00, 13.00–16.00 Mon–Fri

🅐 Staroměstské nám. 5 ☎ 224 861 476 🕐 09.00–18.00 Mon–Fri,
10.00–17.00 Sat, 10.00–15.00 Sun; out of season: 09.00–18.00
Mon–Fri, 10.00–15.00 Sat

   Prague Information Service, or **PIS** (☎ 221 714 444 🌐 www.pis.cz
🕐 Info line: 09.00–12.00, 13.00–16.00 Mon–Fri) has several offices
around town:

🅐 Malostranské mostecké věže (Lesser Town Bridge Towers,
see page 96) 🕐 10.00–18.00 summer only

🅐 Praha Hlavní Nádraží (railway station, see page 49) 🕐 09.00–19.00
Mon–Fri, 09.00–16.00 Sat & Sun, summer; 09.00–18.00 Mon–Fri,
09.00–16.00 Sat & Sun, winter

🅐 Rytířská 31 🕐 10.00–18.00 Mon–Sat, 12.00–16.00 Sun

🅐 Staroměstská radnice (Old Town Hall, see page 65) 🕐 09.00–19.00
Mon–Fri, 09.00–18.00 Sat & Sun, summer; 09.00–18.00 Mon–Fri,
09.00–17.00 Sat & Sun, winter

BACKGROUND READING

Avant-Guide Prague – Insiders' Guide to Progressive Culture by
Dan Levine. A travel-book companion with attitude, and sharp,
insightful commentary on Prague's eateries, shops and clubs.
The Czechs in a Nutshell by Terje B. Englund. A very tongue-in-
cheek look at the Czech national character.
Prague in Black and Gold: The History of a City by Peter Demetz.
An interesting, in-depth look at the history of Prague from
the beginning.
Prague Tales by Jan Neruda. Melancholy stories that only Prague
could inspire.
The Spirit of Prague by Ivan Klíma. A well-constructed collection
relating the ironies and expectations of living in such a
beautiful place.

Emergencies

The following are emergency free-call numbers:

Ambulance ⓘ 155
Dental first aid ⓘ 141 22
Emergency (general number) ⓘ 112
Fire ⓘ 150
First aid ⓘ 141 23
Municipal police ⓘ 156
Pharmacy first aid ⓘ 141 24
Police ⓘ 158

The following telephone numbers are useful if you lose a credit card:

American Express ⓘ 224 194 400
MasterCard and **Eurocard** ⓘ 224 423 135
Visa ⓘ 224 125 353

MEDICAL SERVICES

Emergency treatment and non-hospital first aid are free for all visitors to the Czech Republic. You must pay for any other hospital care up front, but your insurance company will reimburse you when you return from your travels. British and EU nationals receive free health care (but not dental care) through a reciprocal agreement. British travellers should make sure they take their European Health Insurance Card with them.

In an emergency, call 112 and ask for an English-speaking operator. They will determine whether you need an ambulance or a taxi to take you to the nearest health facility. They will also

---

▶ *Prague's skyscape lights up at dusk*

explain your situation to the doctors, so there is no mistaking your condition. Remember to take your passport and some money with you in case you need to have a prescription made out immediately.

Medical centres and clinics
These clinics offer a wide range of medical services in English. Most medical clinics will accept medical insurance and major credit cards, and many have an on-site pharmacy. It's a good idea to make an appointment before your visit; otherwise you could be waiting for hours.

American Dental Associates @ Stará Celnice Building, 2nd Floor Atrium, V Celnici 4/1031 🕿 221 181 121 Ⓦ www.americandental.cz 🕒 Appointments 09.00–17.00 Mon–Fri Ⓝ Metro: Můstek

Canadian Medical Care @ Veleslavínská 1 🕿 235 360 133 Ⓦ www.cmcpraha.cz 🕒 08.00–18.00 Mon, Wed & Fri, 08.00–20.00 Tues & Thur Ⓝ Metro: Dejvická, then tram: 2, 20 or 26 to Nádraží Veleslavín

Health Centre Prague @ Vodičkova 28 🕿 603 433 833 or 603 481 361 Ⓦ www.doctor-prague.cz 🕒 08.00–17.00 Mon–Fri Ⓝ Metro: Můstek

POLICE
Police stations have phone lines open 24 hours a day. The following are the most centrally located:

Police Headquarters @ Jungmannovo nam. 9 🕿 974 851 750

   Also:

@ Bartolomějská 14, Old Town 🕿 974 851 700

@ Vlašská 3, Lesser Quarter 🕿 974 851 730

@ Benediktská 1, New Town 🕿 974 851 710

Lost and Found Office @ Karoliny Světlé 5 🕿 224 235 085 Ⓝ Metro: Národní Třída

EMERGENCY PHRASES

Help!	**Fire!**	**Stop!**
Pomoc!	Hoří!	Stop!
Pommots!	*Horzee!*	*Stop!*

Call an ambulance/a doctor/the police/the fire brigade!
Zavolejte sanitku/doktora/policii/požárníky!
Zavoleyteh sanitkoo/doktorah/politsiyee/pozhahrneeckee!

EMBASSIES & CONSULATES

Australian Consulate 🏠 Klimentská ul.10, 6th Floor ☎ 296 578 350
🌐 www.embassy.gov.au 🕐 08.30–17.00 Mon–Thur, 08.30–14.00 Fri
Ⓜ Metro: Florenc

Canadian Embassy 🏠 Muchova 6 ☎ 272 101 800
🌐 www.czechrepublic.gc.ca 🕐 08.30–12.30 & 13.30–16.30 Mon–Fri
Ⓜ Metro: Hradčanská

New Zealand Consulate 🏠 Dykova 19 ☎ 222 514 672 🕐 09.00–13.00
& 14.00–17.30 Mon–Thur Ⓜ Metro: Jiřího z Poděbrad

South African Consulate 🏠 Ruská 65 ☎ 267 311 114 or 271 731 799
🌐 www.dfa.gov.za 🕐 08.30–16.30 Mon–Thu, 08.30–14.00 Fri
Ⓜ Metro: Želívského

United Kingdom Embassy 🏠 Thunovska 14 ☎ 257 402 111
🌐 http://ukinczechrepublic.fco.gov.uk 🕐 07.30–16.00 Mon–Fri,
08.30–16.00 Sat Ⓜ Metro: Malostranská

United States Embassy 🏠 Tržiště 15 ☎ 257 022 000
🌐 http://prague.usembassy.gov 🕐 13.00–16.00 Mon–Thur
Ⓜ Metro: Malostranská

Editorial/project management: Lisa Plumridge
Copy editor: Monica Guy
Layout/DTP: Alison Rayner

The publishers would like to thank the following individuals and organisations for supplying their copyright photographs for this book: Amit Bansal, page 19; Chris Brown, page 79; Choctaw Ridge, page 101; Marc Di Duca, pages 29, 30–1, 63, 99, 144 & 150; Jenni Douglas, page 87; Enrico, page 89; Bruno Girin, page 75; Julia, page 130; Orlando Pinto/ SXC.hu, page 102; Sergio Russo, page 119; Sean, page 35; Oleg Shipov/ Bigstock, page 116; Carolyn Zukowski, pages 5, 7, 25, 37 & 108; Helena Zukowski, pages 83 & 85; Czech Tourism, all others.

Send your thoughts to
books@thomascook.com

- **Found a great bar, club, shop or must-see sight that we don't feature?**
- **Like to tip us off about any information that needs a little updating?**
- **Want to tell us what you love about this handy little guidebook and more importantly how we can make it even handier?**

Then here's your chance to tell all! Send us ideas, discoveries and recommendations today and then look out for your valuable input in the next edition of this title.

Email the above address (stating the title) or write to: pocket guides Series Editor, Thomas Cook Publishing, PO Box 227, Coningsby Road, Peterborough PE3 8SB, UK.

WHAT'S IN YOUR GUIDEBOOK?

Independent authors Impartial up-to-date information from our travel experts who meticulously source local knowledge.

Experience Thomas Cook's 165 years in the travel industry and guidebook publishing enriches every word with expertise you can trust.

Travel know-how Thomas Cook has thousands of staff working around the globe, all living and breathing travel.

Editors Travel-publishing professionals, pulling everything together to craft a perfect blend of words, pictures, maps and design.

You, the traveller We deliver a practical, no-nonsense approach to information, geared to how you really use it.

Useful phrases

English	Czech	Approx pronunciation
BASICS		
Yes	Ano	*Annoh*
No	Ne	*Neh*
Please	Prosím	*Prosseem*
Thank you	Děkuji	*Dekooyee*
Hello	Ahoj	*Ahoy*
Goodbye	Nashledanou	*Nazhlehdano*
Excuse me	Promiňte	*Prohminyteh*
Sorry	Pardon	*Pardohn*
That's okay	Prima	*Preemmah*
I don't speak Czech	Nemluvím česky	*Nehmlooveem czehskee*
Do you speak English?	Umíte anglicky?	*Oomeeteh anglitskee?*
Good morning	Dobrý den	*Dobree den*
Good afternoon	Dobré odpoledne	*Dobreh odpoledneh*
Good evening	Dobrý večer	*Dobree vecher*
Goodnight	Dobrou noc	*Dobrow nots*
My name is ...	Jmenuji se ...	*Menooyi sch ...*
NUMBERS		
One	Jedna	*Yednah*
Two	Dvě	*Dvyeh*
Three	Tři	*Trzhee*
Four	Čtyři	*Chteerzee*
Five	Pět	*Pyet*
Six	Šest	*Shest*
Seven	Sedm	*Sehdoom*
Eight	Osm	*Ohsoom*
Nine	Devět	*Devyet*
Ten	Deset	*Dessett*
Eleven	Jedenáct	*Yeddenahtst*
Twelve	Dvanáct	*Dvannahtst*
Fifty	Padesát	*Padehsaht*
One hundred	Sto	*Stoh*
SIGNS & NOTICES		
Airport	Letiště	*Letishtye*
Railway station	Železniční stanice	*Zheleznichnee stanyeetseh*
Platform	Nástupiřiště	*Naastuhpeesteh*
Smoking/No smoking	Kuřáci/Zákaz kouření	*Koorzhatsi/zahkas kowrzheny*
Toilets	Záchody	*Zahkhodee*
Ladies/Gentlemen	Dámy/Páni	*Dahmee/Pahnee*
Metro/tram/bus	Metro/tramvaj/autobus	*Metro/tramvay/aootohboos*